The Story of

CHINESE
ZEN

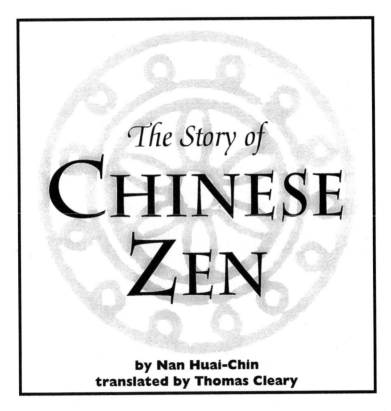

The Story of

CHINESE
ZEN

by Nan Huai-Chin
translated by Thomas Cleary

Charles E. Tuttle Co., Inc.
Boston • Rutland, Vermont • Tokyo

Published by Charles E. Tuttle Company, Inc. of Rutland, Vermont, and
Tokyo, Japan, with editorial offices at 153 Milk Street, Boston,
Massachusetts 02109

Library of Congress Cataloging-in-Publication Data

Nan, Huai-chin.
     The story of Chinese Zen / by Nan Huai-chin.
          p.   cm.
     ISBN 0-8048-3050-9
     1. Zen Buddhism—China. 2. Buddhism—China—History.
3. China—Civilization—Zen influences. I. Title.
BQ9262.9.C5N39 1995
294.3'927'0951—dc20   95–23255
                                                             CIP

First Edition
1 3 5 7 9 10 8 6 4 2

Cover design by Fran Skelly
Printed in the United States of America

Contents

About the Author

Zen Master Nan Huai-Chin was born on March 18, 1918, to a scholar-class family in Luo Ching, in China's Zhejiang province. During his childhood he was extensively tutored in the Chinese classics, and by age seventeen had mastered both Confucian and Taoist works. Although the imperial examination system had been by that time abandoned, the surviving examiner remarked that his literary essays would have ranked him among the top three candidates in the exam.

In his youth, Nan Huai-Chin studied the Chinese martial arts, including swordsmanship, and at eighteen became the provincial martial arts champion. His studies at that time also included Chinese literature, poetry, and calligraphy, as well as the *I Ching* and Chinese medicine. To this day, he remains one of the world's few experts skillful at diagnosing and correcting imbalances of the body revealed through meditation exercises. Master Nan continually sought out a variety of Buddhist, Taoist, and other masters when young, and studied under a total of thirty-two major masters as well as many minor adepts. Following Chinese tradition, much of the great knowledge he received was never written, but only handed down orally from masters to worthy students.

At age twenty-one, Nan became a military commander in the border regions of Szechuan, Yunnan, and Sikang, responsible for over ten thousand men. In 1942, at age twenty-four, he met his enlightened teacher, Zen Master Yuan Huan Hsien, and gave up his military position, with its accompaniments of money, fame, and power, to devote his energies fully to meditation and the search for answers about the questions of life and the universe. Under his teacher's guidance he achieved awakening and later went into retreat for three years at Mount O-Mei in Szechuan Province. During this time he remained secluded in a room, his back to a cliff, and verified his experiences against the entire Buddhist canon, which normally takes many years to read.

In 1945, Nan traveled to Tibet to learn further from the masters of the Esoteric school of Buddhism. There, the Hutukto (Living Buddha) Kung Ka of the White Sect also verified his Zen enlightenment and gave him the additional title of Esoteric Dharma Master. This marked him as one of the few multidisciplinary experts on the cultivation schools of Confucianism, Zen, Taoism, and Esoteric Buddhism, and his writings have therefore often been compared with those of the Great Masters of the Ming and T'ang dynasties. What particularly shows through Nan's writings is his lifelong striving to verify the findings of the sutras and sages. Due to his vast learning, personal experiences in meditation, and interaction with countless Zen practitioners, he has much wisdom to relate to the modern audience.

Master Nan settled in Taiwan in 1947 and was sought out by many students from all walks of life who appreciated his nonsectarian approach to self-cultivation. He has been a teacher, publisher, professor of philosophy at Furen and other Taiwanese universities, philanthropist, and sometimes hermit. His first book, *The Sea of Zen*, was published in 1956, and his *Confucian Analects* is often used in Taiwanese schools as the basic textbook on Confucius. Altogether he has published over thirty books on Zen, Confucianism, Taoism, history, military strategy, and traditional Chinese culture, and over one million copies of his works have been sold in mainland China alone.

Master Nan now resides in Hong Kong where he is involved in various business affairs, such as directing the construction of the first private railway in China, as well as with efforts to reintroduce into China cultural concepts previously destroyed by the Cultural Revolution. Only a few of his books are available in English. This volume, selected and translated by Thomas Cleary, comprises the first half of his Chinese work *Zen and Tao*.

Bill Bodri
Editor

PART I
Background

A Chronology of the Chinese Dynasties

Hsia 2206–1766 BC

1200	
1100	Shang 1766–1123
1000	
900	Western 1122–770
800	Western and
700	Eastern Chou 1122–256
600	*Spring and Autumn Era* 722–484
500	
400	Eastern 770–256
300	*Warring States* 403–221
200	Ch'in 221–206
100	Former or Western 206 BC–8 AD
BC	Han 206 BC–
AD	220 AD
100	Latter or Eastern 25 AD–220
200	
300	Three Kingdoms 220–265: Wei 219–264; Shu-Han 221–263; Wu 221–280
400	Chin 265–419
500	Northern and Southern 420–588
600	Sui 588–618
700	
800	T'ang 618–905
900	
1000	Five Dynasties 906–960
1100	Northern and
1200	Southern Sung 960–1276
1300	
1400	Yüan (Mongol) 1276–1367
1500	Ming 1376–1644
1600	
1700	
1800	Ch'ing (Manchu) 1644–1911
1900	
1950	Republican 1912–1949
	People's Republic of China 1949–

CHAPTER 1

Connections Between Buddhism and Historical Chinese Culture

When we talk about the relationship between Buddhism and the history of Chinese culture, we should first discuss the general outline of Chinese cultural development, which can be divided into three general stages.

The first stage is from around the time of the three prehistorical emperors, Fu Hsi, Shen-nung, and Huang Ti, in approximately the third millennium B.C. Traditional Chinese culture has its remote roots in Fu Hsi's invention of the eight trigrams and the establishment of the cultural thought of the *I Ching*, which embodied concepts on the meeting point of heaven and humanity. The thoughts embedded in the *I Ching* therefore became the basic foundation of Chinese culture.

This primitive culture was simple and unaffected, scientific yet philosophical. It originated from the influence of the three legendary emperors, but further developed under the successive influence of the three imperial dynasties of Hsia (2206–1766 B.C.), Shang (1766–1123 B.C.), and Chou (1122 B.C.–256 A.D.). During this period the Chinese developed philosophies on the interaction of the celestial and the human centered on concepts found in the *I Ching* and the *Book of Etiquette.*

The second stage in cultural development came about as a diversification of the traditional culture. The transitional period between the Chou and Ch'in dynasties (sixth to third centuries B.C.) produced the scholarship and philosophies of many thinkers with mutual differences and similarities. Chinese culture received this influence and then passed through various developments and changes due to the Ch'in and Han dynasty periods (late third century B.C. to early third century A.D.). During this time there gradually evolved the particular forms of three schools of thought: Confucianism, Taoism, and Mo-ism.

The third stage of Chinese cultural development resulted from its passing through the influences of the Wei, Chin, and the Northern and Southern dynasties (third to sixth centuries A.D.). These produced a phase during the Sui and T'ang dynasties (late sixth to early tenth centuries A.D.) and thereafter in which Confucianism, Buddhism, and Taoism stood separately, changing with the times and alternately flourishing and declining.

From this point on, when we talk about Chinese culture through the Sung (960–1276), Yuan (1276–1367), Ming (1367–1644), and Ch'ing (1644–1911) dynasties, it is mainly represented by the three philosophies of Confucianism, Buddhism, and Taoism acting in concert. This phenomenon is like the river basins of Chinese geography:

in the north there is the Yellow River, in the center there is the Yangtze River, and in the south there is the Pearl River Basin.

The interweaving of the Buddhist, Confucian, and Taoist systems has similarly irrigated and enriched the cultural life of China, so it really will not do to talk about any one of these schools in isolation. For those of us who are Chinese, it is all the more imperative that we understand what our own culture is really like. In particular, we have to note that the philosophical thought of China is basically very different from that of Western cultures. If we say that China has philosophical thought, that does not mean that it is an independent specialty, such as it is in the West. In Chinese culture, literature and philosophy have always been inseparable, literature and history are inseparable, and theory and application are inseparable.

Therefore, it goes without saying that in researching Chinese philosophy or Buddhism, from start to finish it is not possible to separate either topic from the four fields of history, literature, philosophy, and politics. The fact that these fields are inseparable is equivalent to the inextricable relationships found among Western philosophy, religion, natural science, and political science. This complex interrelationship is a marvelous example of "different songs sung equally well."

Based on the foregoing points, if you really want to understand the relative ups and downs of Confucian and Taoist doctrines and thought during and after the Ch'in and Han dynasties, as well as the causes and results arising from the importation of Buddhist culture into China, it is necessary to understand the reasons behind the evolution of thought and scholarship in the two Han dynasties: the Former or Western Han (206 B.C.–A.D. 8) and Latter or Eastern Han (A.D. 25–220). The scholarship and thought of both Han dynasties consisted entirely of two realms of thought—Confucian and Taoist. Mo-ist thought had already merged itself into a subsidiary of these two realms by the early part of the Han period, so it had no independent domain at all.

Because of government leadership and social trends, it was Taoist thought that was most popular in the first part of the Western Han period. In the historically famous reigns of Emperor Wen (179–156 B.C.) and Emperor Ching (156–140 B.C.), the whole cultural tendency leaned toward the Huang-Lao arts of Taoism, which were a combination of the teachings of Lao Tzu and the Yellow Emperor Huang-ti. This was due to the needs of the times, and in principle was an inevitable trend in early Han politics.

From this point onward, Taoist learning and thought formed a regular pattern in Chinese history. Whenever disorder or rebellion arose, it has always been necessary to use the guidance of Taoist learning to restore peace. When peace returned to the land, the governing strategy was to use Huang-Lao (Taoism) inwardly while making an outward show of the arts of Confucianism. Since the time of the Western Han period, because of the popularity of Taoist learning and thought, the schools of Legalism, the schools of Yin and Yang, and other schools of thought (such as the Syncretists) all sought rapprochement with the Taoists, gradually flourishing by cleaving to it like parasites. Then, as a product of the degeneracies that built up, an atmosphere of superstition was created in the Western Han period, centered on the concepts of the five elements advanced by the Yin-Yang schools and the practice of divination (fortune-telling). For instance, the rebellion of Wang Mang, who briefly overthrew and supplanted the Han dynasty in the early first century A.D., the restoration of Han rule by Emperor Kuang-wu (r. A.D. 24–57), and the events around the end of Han period and the era of the Three Kingdoms (219–264 A.D.), without exception embodied the psychological elements of political order and disorder formulated in the context of concepts of divination.

Thus it came about that eremitical thinking arose among Taoists at the close of the Han dynasty, which, combined with ideals of chivalry derived from Mo-ism, produced the fledgling forms of Taoist religion. Religious Taoism and Buddhist learning then tried to push each other aside, yet they also absorbed each other's influence. At the same time, the learned thought of the two Han dynasties had transformed the thinking deriving from Confucius, Mencius, and Hsun-tzu into the world of the Han classicist Confucians. This occurred due to the policy of "dismissing all other philosophies and only honoring Confucianism" advocated by Emperor Wu of Han (r. 140–87 B.C.) and the Confucian Tung Chung-shu. As a result, the custom of glossing, annotating, and specializing in one classic tradition filled the courts and countrysides of China.

Because of the interaction of the intellectual authorities, the teachers of classics, and doctors of philosophy with the system of meritocracy, the late Eastern Han dynasty witnessed a growing decadence deriving from hereditary elitism. This led to intrigue, with court eunuchs plotting against scholars, causing learning and thought to interact with political elements in such a way as to foster the development of sources of disorder within the government and society.

7

The early Han dynasty followed the chaos of the Warring States era and the Ch'in regime, so its culture and education were already thoroughly corrupted, but the Western Han work of transmitting the classics and annotating them was really very important. However, from late Eastern Han times, the annotation and transmission of Chinese classics had already become fragmented and tedious. Henceforth, the purpose of learning was to obtain honors, so it became just a tool; if you really wanted to investigate the inner meaning and thought of the culture of the celestial and human, you would find it was already like a listless arrow shot from a spent bow, without even the force to pierce a sheet of paper. Therefore, when the scholarship of the two Han dynasties reached the stage of the Three Kingdoms era, it was already quite lifeless and dull. However, it was precisely at this time that Buddhist scholarship and thought flowed into the country, bringing with it a remarkable new philosophy of profound depth. The forms of scholarship and thought of the Wei (219–264), Chin (265–419), and Northern and Southern dynasties (420–588) took their shape because of this profound influence.

Now as concerns the degeneration and cause of new cultural movements in the Wei, Chin, and Northern and Southern dynasties, ordinarily historians put most of the blame on the sudden upsurge of interest in the Three Arcana (Lao-tzu, Chuang-tzu, and the *I Ching*) and the decadence of the fashion of Pure Conversation, an attempt to talk about the light aspect of matters in an ultrarefined manner. In reality, however, if you understand the evolution of the historical culture of the two Han dynasties, when you address the question as to why people wanted to study the Three Arcana and engage in Pure

Conversation, you cannot attribute the fault to a few scholars such as Ho Yen and Wang Pi who emphasized this style.

In Chinese history, when it came to taking a leading role in the evolution of learning and thought, a small number of intellectuals could certainly start a fashion, but those who really exercised the power were always members of the political leadership. When Confucius promoted reverence for the ancient sage leaders Yao, Shun, Yu, T'ang, Wen, Wu, and the Duke of Chou, this was surely the case; and the question of whether or not the direction of leadership in later ages was correct can be no exception either.

The rulers and ministers of the early T'ang dynasty (618–905), taking the lead in learning and thought, are the ones who opened the way for the development of the Buddhist and Taoist religions in China. The rulers and ministers of the early Sung dynasty took the lead in promoting Confucianism to give birth to the Study of Inner Design school of thought. The same thing also happened later in the Ming and Ch'ing dynasties. In all cases, it was the support from the rulers and ministers that made possible the evolution of Chinese culture. So if you say that the changes in scholarly fashions are due to one or two people, you can be sure that this is not something that can be done by men of idle words who sit around holding discussions in endless conferences.

In sum, when we look closely at the history of the development of the Three Arcana studies and the fashion of Pure Conversation in Wei and Chin times, we find that their imbalances were not the fault of the philosophies of Lao-tzu and Chuang-tzu; nor were they errors of Buddhist *prajna* teachings that discuss emptiness and subtlety. From a close reading of history, one discovers that these imbalances were actually due to the influence of the literary sentiments of Emperor Wu of Wei (Ts'ao Ts'ao) and his sons. As to Ho Yen and Wang Pi, who delved into the Three Arcana studies, both were young aristocrats used to privilege and were arrogant and haughty: they could not pursue a kind of scholarship that involved purity and quietude, precision and subtlety, and they could not practice the kind of mental work that produced penetrating comprehension and far-reaching knowledge. Yet they used the stylish exterior of the Lao-Chuang philosophy to annotate the Three Arcana.

This was an inevitable result, both literarily and philosophically; so if we look at the thought of the Wei, Chin, and the Northern and Southern dynasties from the standpoint of pure philosophy, with the exception of Buddhist studies we find that the so-called study of the Three Arcana was only literary and philosophical. This study of mystical arcana turned into the fashion of Pure Conversation, and Pure Conversation produced the idea of the "use of uselessness," relegating all affairs of state to the status of mere scenery of the passing seasons. This was an inevitable result of the trend of events.

As for Buddhist learning and thought at this same time, during the Eastern and Western Chin dynasties and the Northern and Southern dynasties, Central Asian people rose up and entered the central plain of China, competing among themselves for hegemony. This allowed the great flow of Buddhism eastward to continue unbroken, thus establishing a foundation for Chinese Buddhism and the development of Chinese Buddhist doctrine in the Sui (588–618) and T'ang dynasties that occurred afterward.

Some consider the importation of Buddhist doctrine

into China during the Northern and Southern dynasties to have been based on the armed invasions of Central Asian peoples, in the same way that Western religions proselytized in China at the end of the Manchurian-ruled Ch'ing dynasty. However, this issue is very clear in Chinese historical materials: the two situations cannot be equated. In reality, when Central Asian peoples invaded China during the Northern and Southern dynasties, their cultural base was too shallow and slight, and they basically had no culture or philosophy to speak of. They had no concern with religion and politics; they were just a bunch of ignorant, barbaric plunderers.

Later, however, the deeds of the likes of Shih Yen and Yao Ch'in were somewhat restrained in their wantonness and destructiveness entirely because they were affected by the influence of Buddhist teaching. Another example is the situation under the Northern Wei dynasty, which absorbed Confucian and Taoist culture as a result of Buddhist influence. This is clearly documented in history, so there should be no argument about it.

In sum, the Buddhism of the Northern and Southern dynasties, by merging with Confucian and Taoist culture, set the stage for the culture of the Sui, T'ang, and subsequent dynasties as well as the upsurge of Buddhist learning in China. Distinguished monks coming to China from Central Asia, people such as Fo-t'u-teng and Kumarajiva, were all men of outstanding brilliance who devoted their energies to Buddhist cultural work throughout their lives. Their contributions to Chinese culture and thought have all been of lasting merit, which no one can deny.

Another person of note was Shen Yueh, who is famous for discovering the science of phonetics and rhyme in China, which came about through his involvement in Buddhist scriptural translation projects. Then there was Liu Hsieh, who developed the science of grammar through Buddhist translation and wrote the famous treatise "Sculpting Dragons in the Heart of Writing." Also, the stone caves at Yun-kang and the T'ang dynasty murals at Tun-huang, as well as music, poetry and song, fine arts, and other developments, all had some connection with Buddhism.

However, it must be remembered that from the time of the Eastern Han dynasty to the Sui and T'ang eras, Indian Buddhist thought was absorbed to produce the characteristics of Chinese Buddhist culture and went through many trials and tribulations, an intricate and complex process taking about four or five hundred years before it finally developed into the culture of the T'ang dynasty. So being familiar with the old and knowing the new, when we modern people want to talk about the interpenetration and fusing of Chinese and Western cultures, even though the times have changed and conditions are different (and also taking into consideration the development of modern science and technology) we must realize that in no way can this fusion happen within a short period of time; it may take a century for it to be consummated. Therefore, young Chinese intellectuals should be alert and even more diligent in facing up to trends in their culture in the near future, as well as to the responsibility they personally bear for the country, its people, its history, and its culture.

As to the development of the presentations of Confucian, Buddhist, and Taoist learning from the Sui and T'ang dynasties onward, this naturally had its own historical background. The remote causes behind this development are as I have already set forth above, but the proximate causes show an additional facet.

First, because of the connection with the Li clan, which was the ruling house of the T'ang dynasty, from the time of the T'ang Emperor T'ai-tsung (r. 627–649) Taoism became officially established as the national orthodoxy, honoring Li Lao-chun as the founder of the religion. Thus Taoism was established on the foundation of the polity and education of the T'ang dynasty.

Second, the rulers and ministers of the T'ang dynasty were deeply interested in Buddhism, even though they honored Taoism. Thus, in reality Buddhism and Taoism were both respected, and distinctions were made only in terms of the ranking of their personnel, that is all.

Third, from the beginning, many of the generals and ministers involved in founding the T'ang dynasty were students of the school of the literatus Wang T'ung, whose teaching took after the best in the doctrines and philosophies of Confucianism, Buddhism, and Taoism without drawing boundaries between them. Because of this, the general run of literati, the Confucian intellectuals, mostly held philosophies in which Confucianism and Buddhism were not divided, and Confucianism and Taoism were not distinguished.

So it was that after the mid-T'ang dynasty period, although the master calligrapher and famous essayist Han Yu (who was considered an orthodox Confucian) stirred up a notorious anti-Buddhist affair, in reality the pros and cons of this case were exaggerated by people of later times. Upon careful reading of Han Yu's anti-Buddhist writings as well as investigating the historical facts, we find that at that time he was just dissatisfied with the

Buddhist institution and a certain type of Buddhist; he did not attack Buddhism itself very much.

Furthermore, after Han Yu, the most powerful reason why the Confucians of the schools of Inner Design during the Sung, Yuan, Ming, and Ch'ing dynasties repudiated Buddhism was their claim that Buddhism rejected social norms due to its monastic system, in which neither familial nor political authority are recognized. Other than this, there were a few criticisms concerning Buddhism, but all of them were the uninformed opinions of outsiders and are not worthy of serious consideration.

From a more profound point of view, Han Yu's historical repudiation of Buddha caused no loss to Buddhism, so very few of the eminent monks and Zen masters of the time came forward to speak on the matter. We should note here that those who really strike criticism at the very being of a religion are often themselves originally members of that religion. That is the rule, past and present, in China and elsewhere: people of all religions should examine it deeply.

The upsurge in Buddhist studies during the T'ang dynasty influenced every aspect of Chinese culture, later reaching Japan and the countries of the East. There were three main reasons for this. First, the land was at peace and society was stable; talented Buddhists were therefore able to appear one after another to found the doctrines and principles of the various schools of Chinese Buddhism, thus influencing all of Chinese culture and education in the T'ang dynasty.

Second, the fashions of the Zen schools—the Southern school of sudden enlightenment and the Northern school of gradual enlightenment—spread everywhere, expanding vastly. Like honey in water, like salt

adding flavor, the literature and cultural studies of the
T'ang dynasty became everywhere filled with the living
potential of Zen consciousness. At the same time, Zen
Master Pai-chang established the communal monastic system in China, causing the ten schools of Buddhist studies
to take shelter under one order. This established the special character of Chinese Buddhism and Chinese Buddhist
studies, which set a shining example for all times and all
nations.

Third, Dharma Master Hsuan-tsang returned to
China from his studies in India. The influence of his work
translating Buddhist scriptures for China, and the com-
pletion of the translation of Buddhist literature on the
doctrines of Consciousness Only and phenomenal characteristics, enabled the religious and philosophical thought
within Chinese culture to firmly establish a comprehensive
system of thought. Thus Buddhism could get along with
Confucianism and Taoism, absorbing and recasting the
best of all philosophies, forming the particular characters
of the three great streams of Chinese culture. These are the
three reasons why Buddhism spread widely during the
T'ang dynasty.

When beings peak in power, they wane; when things
come to an extreme, they change. Therefore, the transformation and change in the direction of Buddhist studies
and the Zen schools that came after the late T'ang and
the Five dynasties period (906–960) were inevitable
trends in cultural history. Once the beginning of the Sung
dynasty had arrived, the founding rulers and ministers
revered the doctrines of Confucius and Mencius, and at
this point the literati (who were of course Confucian
intellectuals) semiconsciously absorbed the spirit and
methods developed in Buddhist studies and practice over

the preceding four hundred years (since the Sui and T'ang dynasties). This stirred them to change, and they produced four schools on the study of Inner Design.

The educational methods and manners of the Study of Inner Design schools, as well as the scope of their library system, were all adapted from the formats of the Zen schools. Speaking objectively, one would have to say that the Inner Design Studies of the Sung and Ming dynasties were equivalent to a Confucianist Zen, whereas the Zen school of Buddhism was like Buddhist Confucianism and Taoism. In actuality, this similarity is not to be overestimated, since it just refers to their outward forms. If we investigate the differences and similarities among their real contents, we find considerable distinctions.

Having gone through two or three hundred years of mutual struggle for supremacy through the Northern and Southern Sung dynasties, when Zen Buddhism and Inner Design Studies came to their latter days, they both tended to decline at the same time. Zen Buddhism was adulterated by the false Zen of "silent illumination" (keeping silent) and "crazy Zen," whereas in Inner Design Studies there arose the controversy between Chu Hsi and Lu Hsiang-shan on honoring the essence of virtue and pursuing scholarship on the Way.

Once the Yuan dynasty Mongols invaded China militarily, bringing with them the Lamaism of Esoteric Buddhism, this caused the great houses of both Confucianism and Buddhism to produce disconnected, fragmentary weeds and brambles. From this point onward, three centuries of culture and education in the Ming dynasty were trapped within an atmosphere characterized either by Inner Studies of crazy Zen, or by crazy Zen of Inner Studies.

Even though Wang Yang-ming (1472–1529) appeared and founded the genuinely practical doctrine of innate knowledge and innate capacity, nevertheless, because it was neither Confucianism nor Buddhism but something in between, great problems still remained. This caused the great Confucians of the late Ming period to scorn Wang Yang-ming's teaching and hurl the criticisms that "Sages fill the streets," and "Under ordinary conditions they sit quietly and talk about the essence of mind; when they face a crisis they simply die to repay the ruler of the nation," and so on. There certainly was a reason for this criticism; it was not purely an emotional reaction. Although a genuine revival of Buddhist studies and the Zen school occurred in the beginning of China's Ch'ing dynasty, they still were not able to recover from their fall and could not become powerful because the established national policy was to use the foreign cult of Lamaism to control the western and northern borderlands.

To sum up, this simplified and compact introductory exposition should give one a general understanding of the important points in the causes and conditions of the cultural history of Buddhism and China. This synopsis is extremely terse, with many details and explanations absent because we are only introducing the flavor of overall trends. Don't be disheartened if the names of dynasties, personalities, and philosophical movements seem a little too much at present. To become a specialist in the history and influence of the Zen school in China would require deep familiarity with all of this material, but for the general reader this overview is sufficient.

PART II

A Brief Introduction to
the Contents of Buddhist Study

CHAPTER 2

The Background of Indian Culture

Buddhist study is the content of the teaching established by Shakyamuni Buddha. In Buddhist study, the three concepts of (1) Buddhist teachings, (2) Buddhist principles and methods, and (3) the process of learning Buddhism each have different meanings. Buddhist teachings are the teachings left by the Buddha, which are of a religious nature. Buddhist principles and methods include the philosophical and academic aspects of Buddhist study as well as all its methods of seeking realization. Learning Buddhism means to actually carry out the teachings left by the Buddha, studying in accord with his methods of guidance.

Chinese scholarship has a proverbial saying that "Buddhist study is as vast as the misty ocean," from which one can imagine the richness of its content. So if we are to introduce the important points of Buddhist study simply and very briefly from an academic point of view, we must first understand the cultural background of ancient India.

When we bring up this subject, we have to recognize that for thousands of years Indian culture and thought evolved circuitously in the context of religion and philosophy, and in light of the practical cultivation methods used by various religions and philosophies to attain realization. The teachings in present-day India are no exception. All of India's historical culture has gone through periods of religious struggle, ideological conflict, and inequality among social classes. And when foreign powers invaded the country beginning in the seventeenth century, at all times and in all places they used the contradictions in Indian religious thought as a method of control.

The doctrines of ancient Indian religions, including the religious and philosophical ideologies around the time of Shakyamuni Buddha, were so many and various that they could in fact be a blueprint for a comparative religion and comparative philosophy of the world. Usually discussions of Indian philosophy mention six teachers to explain what the six major schools of philosophy were like, but actually in the translated literature of Chinese Buddhist studies it often says that there were as many as ninety-six different schools of philosophical thought. Although the entire body of information is inadequate, fragmentary accounts still contain much valuable material. However, international discourse on Indian philosophy or Buddhism has been influenced by European academics since the seventeenth century and has never considered Chinese Buddhist resource materials important, thus causing both Chinese and foreign scholars to erase the value of Chinese Buddhist studies with a single stroke. This is very regrettable and indeed lamentable.

In sum, ancient Indian philosophy and religion already addressed all such topics as the existence or nonexistence of a supreme being, monism and pluralism, idealism and materialism, and so on. As far as Buddhism is concerned, by about the middle of the Sung dynasty it had entered completely into China due to the infiltration of foreign teachings, and had become Chinese Buddhism; after that the evolution of Indian cultural history has nothing at all to do with Buddhism. This point calls for special explanation so as to avoid misunderstanding.

The Situations and Political Conditions of Ancient India

The time of Shakyamuni roughly corresponds to China's Spring and Autumn era (722–484 B.C.), but the matter of exactly when he lived has been a bone of contention among Chinese and foreign scholars past and present. From the point of view of world cultural history, at this stage, in the course of no more than a single century of historical evolution in the East and West, welter of confusion that it was, a succession of philosophers emerged, a magnificent array. In China there were people such as Lao-tzu and Confucius, India had Shakyamuni's community of philosophers, and in Greece there were individuals such as Socrates and Plato. All were people whose influence on human civilization was to last for thousands of years.

At that time, China operated under a feudal system, but the Chou dynasty emperor was still at the center of society, honored alone as the supreme head reigning over all the land. India, on the other hand, was at that time divided into hundreds of nation-states contending for power, and had no central authority. Shakyamuni himself was a prince of peerless intelligence: he received his education in a royal palace, and as a youth was broadly learned and multitalented. Because he personally witnessed the ravages of war in India, and observed the pain of the strong devouring the weak in the realm of living beings, he wanted to discover a way of true peace for the masses of the world. So he resolutely left home and traveled all over in search of the teachings left by the philosophers of antiquity, searching for the truth of the universe and human life.

After he left home, he sought out the methods of practice and realization of the traditional teachings of Brahminism, as well as the devotional life of transmundane asceticism practiced by other religions and schools of thought. As a result, he finally realized that none of them was the ultimate learning, so he went through a phase of solitary ascetic practice, cultivating realization on his own. He left home at the age of nineteen, but began to spread his teaching only when he was thirty-two.

Modern scholars treat Shakyamuni the same way they do Confucius: some recognize him as the founder of a religion, others recognize him as a philosopher or educator. But in reality these ranks and positions of honor have no meaning at all for Shakyamuni Buddha. An individual true sage philosopher, he was able to ignore the vainglory of the world; he cast off the honor of royalty as one would throw away a worn shoe, without a second glance. At the same time, he frequently spoke of ancient Buddhas and other Buddhas, so he obviously didn't consider himself the founder of a teaching. It was when it came to the point where his teaching had changed into a religion that he was set up on a jewel throne as the founder of a religion, which was the doing of the followers of second-hand tradition in later generations.

I feel that the founders of all the religions mostly had this kind of heart in them. For example, Lao-tzu was hauled up onto the jewel throne of the founder of Taoism as Lord Lao the Highest, but where in this is the original intent of Lao-tzu's heart as indicated by the saying that "it is not known where he died," or the tale that he left the country riding on a blue ox? Rather than say that Shakyamuni started Buddhism and was the founder of the religion, it would be better to say that he edited and compiled the whole body of ancient traditional culture and thought of India, and brought out its unique and independent spirit of cultural teaching, making it even greater and worthier of savoring.

CHAPTER 3

*The Contribution to Humankind and
the World Made by Shakyamuni's
Leaving Home and Attaining Enlightenment*

N ow let us encapsulate the essential points of Shakyamuni's leaving home, attaining enlightenment, and disseminating his teaching. Overall there are five main points.

Establishing a Magnificent Array of Ways of Guidance, Shakyamuni Taught a Way to Govern Nations with Kindness and Compassion at Heart

Shakyamuni took into consideration the fact that he could have been a peerless hero and governed the whole Indian continent, but even though a hero may be able to conquer the world, he cannot conquer himself. What is more, human history is always in the process of change, and it is impossible to maintain a perpetually unchanging kingship. He wanted to establish a kind of cultural thought that could offer guidance for ten thousand generations; he wanted to conquer himself and fulfill the need to achieve inner wisdom, so he wanted to "detach from feelings and abandon desires, thus to be free from burdens," and consequently he left home to seek enlightenment.

His aspiration was in fact rewarded, and he set up a magnificent array of teachings as methods of guidance, thus winning the respect and reverence of countless generations of people in many nations of the world. In terms of the concept of economic value habitually used by modern-day people, the value of Shakyamuni's work as a perennial teaching for humanity cannot be compared with the value of his possibly having spent his life as a king or an emperor.

Based on the effects of the way of guidance he established, within a few hundred years there emerged the achievements of Ashoka, the great king of India, which constituted the most glorious page of cultured government in that country's history. This paralleled the way the doctrines of Confucius formed the cultured government of the early Western Han dynasty; but when I say paralleled, that does not mean they were the same. Something is connected with the spirit of developmental teaching in the Buddha's various ways of guidance, as well as in the models provided by the behavioral regulations of the Great and Small Vehicles of Buddhism, that corresponds to the *Book of Rites* in traditional Chinese culture, which also encapsules the basic spirit of the philosophy of human etiquette, social duty, and law. Since the time of the T'ang and Sung dynasties, whenever relatively objective scholars draw comparisons between Shakyamuni and Confucius, they recognize that if Confucius had lived in the India of his time, he would have done as Shakyamuni did, and if Shakyamuni had lived in the China of his time, he would have proceeded as did Confucius. As it is said, "For sages of the East and sages of the West, this mind is the same, this principle is the same, and the path is one."

Breaking Up India's Traditional Concept of Caste, Shakyamuni Preached Equality Extending to All Living Beings

Indian history has always been characterized by a very rigid concept of caste. Usually they speak of the first caste as the Brahmin, the traditional priesthood of Brahminism; the second caste is the Kshatriya, the warriors who traditionally held military authority; the third caste is the Vaishya, farmers, herders, merchants, and such people; and the fourth caste is the Shudra, those people involved in menial occupations. After Shakyamuni attained enlightenment, he energetically expounded the idea that the natures and forms of all living beings are equal. Not only did he recognize all humanity as being equal; he also recognized all creatures—whatever has flesh and blood and is conscious, even to the border of the divine and human—as belonging in the category of living beings: in terms of the substance of their basic nature, everyone must originally be equal. So people should not harm others with uncivil and malicious intentions, and at the same time they should not harm any living things out of selfishness.

Human and other living beings partake of the essence of suchness and so are fundamentally equal by nature; that is why everyone can become a Buddha by doing good and getting rid of evil. All living beings, celestial and human, can attain Buddhahood by doing good and eliminating evil. Although the terminology is different, this teaching derives from the same source as the Confucian principle that "the people are my relatives, beings are my companions" and the idea preached by the philosophers of Inner Design Studies that "everyone can be a sage."

The principle of Shakyamuni's teaching on the oneness of others and self, the doctrine of the equality of living beings, may be called an ideology of thoroughgoing egalitarianism that shines gloriously throughout past and present. At the same time he himself set the example. In the community of monks whom he personally guided in their studies, everyone was equal regardless of their social origins; only virtuous conduct was considered important.

Some may assume that once we speak of equality we will come to a point at which right and wrong are not distinguished, where good and bad are not divided. This is not to be misunderstood: what Shakyamuni spoke of was the basic equality of essence (substance) and form (function); when we arrive at the realm of equality, we still need the distinction between good and evil as well as the developmental exercise of doing good and eliminating evil. So the effort to get rid of evil and turn toward good, to depart from evil people and do whatever is good, is indeed an incomparably great virtue. There is no contradiction at all. This too is ultimately much the same in meaning, although different in expression, from the saying of Confucians that "wise kings got angry once and pacified the land."

Synthesizing the Doctrines of Transmigration Found in Ancient Indian Religious Traditions, Shakyamuni Set Up a Phenomenology of Life in Terms of Past, Present, and Future Causes and Effects, with Recurring Cycles of Six Courses of Existence

From the basic idea that "others and self are one, natures and characteristics are equal," and the methodology of doing good and eliminating evil, one arrives at the realm of "one suchness" and "equality," whereupon it becomes a matter of course to delve into the question of the source of the life of living beings. Shakyamuni used the method of generalization to array the species of life into kinds, dividing them into general categories known as the six courses of existence: the celestial course, the *asura* or antigod course (whose realm is on the border of the divine and the demonic), the human course, the animal course, the hungry ghost course, and the hellish course of existence.

Because of the differences in the amounts and degrees of good and bad in their thoughts and actions, all living beings immerse themselves in being phenomena of life right in these six courses. People can do good and be born in heaven, and they can also do evil and turn into animals or hungry ghosts, or even fall into hell. But if celestial beings forget goodness, stir their thoughts, and do something wrong, they can also turn into antigods, or even go off into other courses of existence. At this point it is recognized that the phenomena of the life of all living beings in this universe, those that are different and those that are the same, all interchange through the good and bad in a single thought formulated in the mind. This is similar to the Taoist theory of the evolving universe. (But note that similar does not mean entirely the same.)

So the good and bad in a thought, and the action of rousing the mind and stirring thoughts, build up the subtle bit by bit to develop into the manifestly obvious. So Shakyamuni formulated the theory of cause and effect in three time frames: past, present, and future. Past causes build up into present effects, and the implications of present causes will build up into future effects. So the future and the past are like an endless ring, and the expression of recurring cycles of transmigration refers to this cyclical movement. Then he set up a doctrinal system of past, present, and future causes and effects, with recurring cycles of the six courses of existence. This is similar to the concept of causes and effects of virtue expressed in the *I Ching*: "A home that accumulates goodness will surely have abundant felicity," and "If goodness is not accumulated, it is insufficient to establish one's name; if evil is not accumulated, it is insufficient to destroy one's person."

Shakyamuni Pioneered Views of the Universe and the World

Whenever the ancient religions and philosophies of India approached metaphysical problems, they naturally touched on the search for the meeting point of the celestial and the human. Although the ultimate ends of their ideas and doctrines all came down to getting into Heaven, the Heaven worshiped by each individual sect and school was different, with no unity among them, and in addition there existed a clash between ideas of monotheism and pantheism.

The doctrine of Shakyamuni synthesized the borders of the celestial and the human into three zones (the "three realms") called the realms of desire, of form, and the formless realm. The realm of desire stretches from the celestial inhabitants in the heavens of our solar system to the humans, animals, hungry ghosts, and denizens of hell below.

The expression "realm of desire" indicates that the life of the beings in this realm comes from craving (for sex and nourishment). Speaking in a broad sense, craving includes the pleasures of the five desires for form, sound, fragrance, flavor, and feeling. In a narrow sense, it involves the acts of smiling, looking, conversing, embracing, and touching.

The realm of desire has six levels of celestial realms; for instance, the one among them called the Trayastrimsha Heaven contains an array of thirty-three heavens that alternate in prominence according to the time. The human realm within the realm of desire is generally divided into the four sectors—east, west, north, and south. Our human world is in the southern sector known as Jambudvipa. The overall name of this world is Saha, which has a double meaning: endurance and sorrow. This refers to the fact that this world is full of sorrow, with much that is painful and difficult; and yet humans and all living beings not only can endure that sorrow, suffering, and hardship, but can diligently turn toward good, thereby becoming worthy of praise. If there were no sorrow or suffering in the world, we naturally could not distinguish good or bad. Fundamentally, there is no good or bad to speak of, so it should be the completeness of nature that is considered good; then nothing can be totally denied, and nothing can be praised.

Each of the celestial and human worlds in the realm of desire has a ruler. Beyond the realm of desire is the realm of form, where the beings experience only feelings and ideas, without desires. The beings in the realm of form can produce the fruit of life just by looking at each other and smiling in a meeting of minds. In that realm are eighteen levels of heavens corresponding to states of realization produced by beings cultivating the realms of quiet contemplation and meditative concentration. The highest heaven in the realm of form is called the Heaven of the Ultimate of Form, whose ruler is the god Mahesvara.

Beyond the realm of form is the formless realm, which is reckoned to have four levels of heavens. Those who have attained the fruits of practicing meditation are born in the formless realm where they have only mental consciousness; emotional desires do not exist for them. Finally, the one governing this whole domain of three realms is called the great god Brahma.

From this simple explanation it can be seen how Shakyamuni partitioned the spheres of the celestial and human into a general scheme of sixty heavens under the overall rubric of the three realms, all of which are still within the bounds of the recurring cycles of the six courses of existence. This cosmic world of three realms has an individual solar system as its primary unit. And stretching from the human world up to the sun and moon, and the heavens within the three realms, the realities and concepts of time have their own individual differences. For example, a day and night on the moon is equal to a fortnight in the human world; a day and night on the sun is equal to a year in the human world. Differentiated in this way, the time frames of the worlds of the cosmos are so many and so detailed as to be incalculable, but in sum it can be said that Shakyamuni's view of the universe was that of an infinitely vast cosmos.

In his worldview, with one solar system as a basic world system unit, a world system of a thousand solar systems was called a thousand-world system. A group of a thousand thousand-world systems was called a million-world system. A group of a thousand million-world systems was called a billion-world system. Shakyamuni said that in this limitless, boundless cosmos there are innumerably many such billion-world systems, as many as there are grains of sand in the Ganges River. When from this perspective we look back upon the tumultuous agitation of lustful beings in the human world, it appears pathetically small and trivial.

Shakyamuni expounded his view of the cosmos in terms of three realms containing billions of world systems, thus synthesizing the various ancient Indian religious and philosophical concepts of the divine and the human. He also opened up the domain of the heart of human knowledge, reaching worlds inaccessible even to astronomy and mathematics, and in the other direction analyzing matter all the way to the subatomic level, entering so deeply as to reach the ultimately formless and signless subtlety. Thus he made it hard for the contents of the philosophical thought of any school, past or present, to compare with his for richness and completeness.

Shakyamuni Synthesized a Metaphysical Ontology

The controversies of ancient Indian religious philosophies and various sects of philosophical thought with regard to the source of life in the universe are not only a welter of diverse doctrines without a unifying agreement as to what is right, but they also each construct a system of doctrine based on logic. These doctrines, however, never go beyond the bounds of theism and atheism, monism and pluralism, idealism and materialism.

In reality, if we sum up the most basic and fundamental searches of human culture throughout the world and its history, they are still not beyond these few questions. For thousands of years the human race has addressed the question most personal to humankind itself, the question of the source of life: from religion to philosophy and from philosophy to science, humanity has been seeking, wandering in bewilderment, arguing and debating. When you look at it, it is really a great parody of human culture.

In the search for the truth about the universe, human life, and life in general, each ancient Indian religious philosophy had its own views and its own methods of gaining peace of mind and defining its fate, and each thought it had already attained the ultimate way to pure liberation. Some thought the final union of the soul with the great Brahma is the supreme Way; others thought extinction of desires and thoughts is the ultimate. Some considered the Great Way to be maintaining the clarity of the soul without using sense awareness, keeping spiritual awareness without using thought. And then there were also those who believed that when a person dies it is like a lamp going out, so the real truth is just to see to enjoyment of pleasure in the present. Some even considered themselves to already have attained the nirvana that is the realm of ultimately pure liberation. There were so many various opinions that they cannot all be mentioned.

Addressing these problems as he expounded his teaching, Shakyamuni drew his conclusions through a process of synthesizing, harmonizing, and adapting. He considered all phenomena in the cosmos having life to be born of a combination of causes and conditions, without any single ruling function therein: they come into being when the conditions arise, and disappear when the conditions are gone.

So the highest (or ultimate, or primal) function of the life of the cosmos is that in which mind and matter are the same substance. If you look at it from the point of view of religious concepts, or from the angle of the sacred, it could be called Buddha, or God, or Lord, or Spirit, or some other transpersonal spiritual sacred epithet. If you look at it from the angle of reason, it could also be called essence, or mind, or principle, or natural law, or the realm of reality, and so on. If you look at it from the angle of conceptions customary among humankind, you could also call it something like a spiritual body, in the sense of an inexhaustible spiritual body at the root source of life. In sum, speaking in terms of substance, it has emptiness as its substance; speaking in terms of characteristics, the forms of all that exists in the cosmos are its characteristics; speaking in terms of function, all actions of all things and all beings in the cosmos are its function.

Metaphorically speaking, it is like an ocean: the waves arising in the ocean water are like the worlds of the cosmos produced by causes and conditions; while the bubbles of foam on the waves are like the individual bodies of living beings, each with its own particular form produced by causes and conditions. Although the phenomena of the waves and the bubbles have their individual dissimilarities, they are never apart from the single inherent nature of water. But a metaphor is just a similitude, not the essence of the thing itself.

Living beings, because they cannot experientially arrive at the ultimate end of the fundamental substance of their own nature, thus abandon the root and pursue the branches, each clinging to their own views, their own knowledge, considering it to be the ultimate. Thus it is that sentient beings rest on their own subjectivity to formulate different knowledge and opinions of the world.

But in reality, subjectivity and objectivity both belong to the discriminating function of thinking consciousness; and the knowledge and perception of thinking consciousness itself functions in dependence on the causes and conditions of the body and the material world, so they themselves are unreal and cannot sufficiently determine the existence or nonexistence of truth. If only people could practice meditation with the thinking consciousness in their own minds quieted, gradually they could realize that the functions of body and mind are changing and inconstant, like the world of phenomena, deceptive and unreal. Seeking progress step by step from this point, analyzing layer by layer, finding out all about human nature and the nature of all things, arriving at the unique body of suchness in which body, mind, and the cosmos are calm and unperturbed, not dwelling in existence, not falling into voidness, one can then realize the primal and ultimate truth of the cosmos and human life.

Shakyamuni called that "true suchness," or the "nirvanic essence," or the "essence of the matrix of the realization of suchness," or "come from suchness." In a broad sense, these are different names for the basic substance of cosmic life. Therefore he recognized that it is not ultimately true to call it either void or existent. There is only one way, which is to arrive at physical and mental stillness and silence, and then seek realization within this stillness and silence. However, that basic substance of cosmic life is inconceivable. "Inconceivable" is a technical term used in the context of methods for cultivating realization; it means that the object cannot be arrived at by ordinary conscious thought or deliberation. So this term "inconceivable" is not to be misunderstood as meaning "unthinkable."

CHAPTER 4

Mahayana Buddhism and Hinayana Buddhism

The contents of Shakyamuni's thought that I have spoken of are the overall essentials of what is generally called Buddhist studies. In Buddhist studies, it is usually customary to distinguish in terms of Mahayana (Great Vehicle) and Hinayana (Small Vehicle); in Chinese Buddhist studies and Buddhism, the Mahayana and Hinayana stand side by side, but the comparatively greater inclination is toward the Mahayana. Buddhist studies currently popular in the West mostly concentrate on the Hinayana, recognizing it as the original Buddhism, and of course the Southern tradition of Buddhism in the countries of Southeast Asia are all based on the Hinayana. To give one a foothold of understanding, in the following discussion I will take a relatively simple route, explaining the Buddhist studies of the Hinayana in terms of three items: philosophy, practice, and methods of seeking realization.

Hinayana Thought

In Hinayana thought, a number of general terms are derived from the analysis of mind and body, such as the five *skandhas,* the three poisons, the twelve faculties and data fields, and the eighteen elements that determine all mental processes. The five *skandhas* are translated in Chinese as the five shadows or five clusters, representing the sense of darkness and accumulation. The five shadows consist of these five items: form, sensation, conception, activity (volition), and consciousness.

The shadow of form includes whatever is visibly manifest, such as color, size, and space, as well as what is not visibly manifest, such as abstractions, hallucinations, and so forth. The word "form" in Chinese sometimes represents sexuality, but in Chinese Buddhism it is very rarely used to represent sexual desire. In sum, the form shadow includes the four gross elements of the physical and biological body: earth (hard substances), water (flowing liquids), fire (the capacity for heat), and wind (vaporization).

The shadow of sensation refers to the biological sense of feeling as well as to psychological reaction. The shadow of conception refers to the thinking function of discursive ideational consciousness. The shadow of activity refers to the kinetic energy of instinctive movement and activity of body and mind. The shadow of consciousness refers to the spiritual substance of mental function.

Because of the basic psychological evils produced by our bodies and minds in association with the world of physical facts and human affairs, there also come to be the so-called three poisons of greed, anger, and folly. The older Buddhist translations, before the Sui and T'ang dynasties, render these three poisons as lust, wrath, and folly. Due to the different evils produced by the three poisons, there are three kinds of psychological evils, which are greed, anger, and folly; four kinds of evils of speech, which are lying, vilification, duplicity, and frivolity; and three kinds of evils of the body, which are murder, theft, and rape.

Having encompassed the functions of the human mind and body under the rubric of five shadows, at the same time Buddhism also distinguishes the relationship between body-mind and the physical world in terms of twelve sense faculties and data fields:

Six Sense Faculties	Six Data Fields
eyes	form/color
ears	sound
nose	odor
tongue	flavor
body	tactile feeling
mind	mind phenomena

Among these, the only one belonging to the sphere of psychology is the thought pattern of the intellect; as for the rest, such as the tactile feelings generated by the body, all are in the realm of biological and physical functions.

Then there are the four truths and twelve causal conditions, which relate to the view of human life and the worldview. The four truths are suffering, accumulation, extinction, and the Way. This says that all in the world of human life is suffering, pure suffering without pleasure, yet beings lack knowledge and take suffering for pleasure. Suffering is generally categorized in terms of eight pains:

birth, old age, sickness, death, not getting what is sought, separation from loved ones, being together with the uncongenial, and flareup of the five shadows. All this is called the truth of suffering.

Because living beings spontaneously pursue passions, they thereby collect and accumulate causes of suffering and so produce suffering as a result, mistaking it for pleasure; this is called the truth of accumulation. If one would extinguish the causes of suffering and the resulting suffering, to arrive at detachment from suffering and enjoyment of bliss, this is called the truth of extinction. Based on this premise, it is inevitable to wish to seek realization of the fruition of the Way, to sublimate human life and attain the ultimate access to reality; this is called the truth of the Way.

Furthermore, since all things and affairs in the human world are changing and unstable, fundamentally lacking in permanent continuity, it is called "impermanent." Because everything in human life is pure suffering without pleasure, it is called "painful." Since all is insubstantial, it is called "empty." Moreover, analyzing the body, mind, and world, we find that there is ultimately no existence of self therein; the so-called world, body, and mind are just supports of self, and are not the reality of self at all, so they are called "selfless." Thus the overall view of the world of human life refers to it as "impermanent," "painful," "empty," and "selfless."

The twelve causal conditions start from ignorance. Ignorance means not understanding the fundamental, not knowing the source. Ordinarily, people are unclear about the origins of human life or the activity of mind and consciousness and do not understand the ultimate. The antithesis of this is to clearly awaken and find out the ultimate, but all living beings come from ignorance, so ignorance is provisionally defined as the first cause.

Activity, the second link in this chain of interdependent relations, arises from ignorance, the primary cause. Activity here means kinetic energy. Third, based on activity there arises the function of consciousness, which is the hidden power of the basic capacity for thought. Fourth, based on consciousness, names (abstract ideas) and forms (concrete biological and physical matter) are constructed. Fifth, based on names and forms, the phenomena of the six sense media are produced. Sixth, based on the six sense media, the feeling of contact arises. Seventh, based on contact, the function of reception in the mind is induced. Eighth, based on reception, the pursuit of cravings arises. Ninth, based on craving, there comes to be a need to grasp. Tenth, based on grasping, the existence of becoming appears. Eleventh, based on becoming, the process of birth takes place. Twelfth, based on birth, is the end result of aging and death. Then, based on aging and death, there is a reentry into ignorance, again forming another causally conditioned life.

Ignorance follows along the order of this cycle of causal conditions as both a cause and an effect, so that repeated birth and destruction are beginningless and endless like a circular ring; falsehood continues, setting up the illusory phenomenon of the process of the world of human life. This didactic model was also used to explain the principles of the physical and temporal extension and continuity of life in the past, present, and future. And if expanded to its fullest implications, it can also be used to interpret time and space.

In sum, the Hinayana Buddhist perspective on the world of human life is just like that of any typical religion, deriving purely from the standpoint of a philosophy of the transmundane, looking on the world as a world of pain and affliction, looking on human life as a life of tragedy and evil, and thus seeking to leave the world, to liberate human life, and to attain pure tranquil nirvana as the fruit of the Way. The praxis and ideology of Hinayana Buddhism are like those of the hermits of Chinese Taoism, biased somewhat like the philosopher Yang Chu; so it had a sort of spiritual affinity with one particular category within Chinese culture and hence was naturally absorbed to become a part of Chinese Buddhism.

The Practice of Hinayana Buddhism

Hinayana practice is based on the three successive studies of discipline, concentration practice, and cultivation of wisdom, ultimately to arrive at liberation and the knowledge and insight of liberation. The rules of discipline contain various different items for monks, nuns, laymen, and laywomen. The basic stipulations of the rules are virtues commonly recognized by humanity, such as not killing, not stealing, not raping, and not lying.

Therefore the function of the Buddhist rules of discipline are very much like the spirit of the *Book of Rites* in Chinese culture, as expressed in the dicta "Do not look at what is improper, do not listen to what is improper, do not say what is improper, do not do what is improper." As for the other detailed regulations, some have to do with manners, and with the self-discipline necessary to prevent subtle and insidious errors. There is also a resemblance to Mo-tzu's lament about "dyeing plain thread with colors," as well as the disciplined frugality of his conduct and the lofty nobility of his aspiration. Except for some of the regulations that vary according to the time and place and are still debatable, really they are a model of virtue purifying the spirit and refining conduct.

Hinayana Methods of Seeking Realization

Hinayana Buddhist methods of seeking realization are mainly based on *dhyana*. The Sanskrit word *dhyana* is sometimes translated into Chinese as "quiet meditation," but this term comes from a paraphrase of the Chinese classic *Ta-hsueh,* or *Great Learning,* where it speaks of knowing, stilling, settling, quieting, stabilizing, meditating, and attaining. Nevertheless, there is some difference.

Dhyana includes both yoga and insight; it is a sort of method of transforming the temperament and training the mind and body. The meditation concentration of Mahayana Buddhism and the meditation of the Ch'an school of later Chinese Buddhism also have differences and similarities.

As to the methods for attaining *dhyana,* some start from the firmness of singleminded faith. Some start from the biological basis of *anapana,* which means tuning the breathing. Some start from the practice of cleaning the mind. Some start from psychological concepts and insights. Some start from mantra or recitation of esoteric writings. The so-called expedient methods for attaining *dhyana* are manifold, but when they are classified overall in terms of the process and order of their practice and realization, they are not beyond four meditations and eight concentrations (*samadhi*). They are also called the nine successive concentrations, nine steps of meditative concentration, or nine *samadhi*. This is because the four meditations and eight stages of concentration can be relabeled in a different fashion, and when the concentration in which senses and perceptions are extinguished is added in, which is the ultimate experience of *arhats* (those who have attained the highest level of Hinayana realization), they are called the nine successive concentrations.

In the first meditation, with one-pointedness of mind, concentration produces joy and bliss. The expression "one-pointedness of mind" refers to the initial accomplishment of using a particular method of cultivation, where one arrives at a state of mind that is calm and quiet. In this state the spirit and thought are unified, focused on one point without any mixed-up thoughts arising and going off on tangents. Gradually a state of biological bliss is induced that is a basic instinct of life itself and not the same as an ordinary feeling of pleasure, and an incomparable psychological joyfulness is attained that is not the same as an ordinary emotional feeling of delight. In the course of proceeding from the first steps of meditation practice to arriving at this stage, one has already passed through what is commonly referred to as the process of opening up the channels of *ch'i* in the body; only then can one arrive at the state of mental calmness and unity.

In the second meditation, one experiences a great joy and bliss from having achieved detachment from life. With progressive cultivation from this point onward, the calm and quiet of the mind become even more solid, and the states of joy and bliss become even more stable. There is the feeling of being liberated from the pain and affliction caused by mental and physical pressure.

The third meditation is characterized by detachment from joy and the experience of bliss. Due to the maturation and stabilization of the experience of the psychological joyfulness previously induced, it becomes a habit that is different from the ordinary, and only the state of bliss remains.

The fourth meditation is characterized by relinquishment, mindfulness, and purity. In the three preceding stages of meditation concentration, the functions of feeling and consciousness still remain. Having arrived at the fourth state, one relinquishes feeling and arrives at a state of incomparable quietude, which is finally the ultimate end.

In addition to these four kinds of meditation state, there are also four states of concentration. Concentration in a state of infinite form refers to attainment of mental and physical calm and quiet in the midst of infinite vistas of light. Concentration in a state of infinite space refers to attaining calm and quiet in a boundless infinity of open awareness. Concentration in a state of infinite consciousness refers to attaining calm and quiet in a spiritual state never before experienced. Concentration in a state of neither thought nor thoughtlessness refers to attaining calm and quiet in a state transcending ordinary sensation and perception. The expression "not thought" means that it is not a state of conscious thought; the expression "not thoughtlessness" means that it is not entirely void of a sense of knowledge through spiritual feeling.

The final type of concentration is extinction, the state of arhats, which is a realm transcending ordinary verbal expression. If we were compelled to give a metaphorical explanation, we might say it is equivalent to a state in which the celestial and the human are merged, united with boundless, formless space. Therefore, the arhats, who have achieved the highest attainment of the

Hinayana, know beforehand when their earthly life is over. When ready to pass away they manifest wonders, "reduce their bodies to ashes and extinguish their knowledge," saying of themselves, "My life is over, my pure conduct is established, my task is done, and I will not experience any further becoming," and then calmly pass away into extinction.

This simple introduction provides a general glimpse into what Hinayana Buddhism is like. First, by way of study and reflection directed toward theoretical understanding, its application starts with the practice of behavioral discipline according to absolute virtues, and arrives at seeking realization of meditation concentration and attainment of liberation. Its final goal recognizes the possibility of escaping from the sphere of birth and death in this world, and permanently abiding in a spiritual state of absolute quiescence and purity.

In reality, is this spiritual state of purity and quiescence the ultimate attainment of the life of the universe? Is it really possible thereby to be liberated from the cycle of birth and death? From the point of view of Mahayana Buddhism, these are very serious problems.

At the same time, the states of *dhyana*, as Shakyamuni also said, are a kind of common phenomenon; that is, they are not the monopoly of Buddhism. As long as they deeply understand the principles and diligently cultivate realization, ordinary worldly people and those of other religions and philosophies can all attain similar states of concentration, but none of them are the ultimate complete teaching. They are concerned only with detachment from the world, seeking their own comfort, to resolve the function of discrete portions of the flow of life. They suppose themselves already to have been liberated from birth and death and to be dwelling in the state of extinction and purity, but they have just fallen into a state of partial emptiness, on a par with self-centered hermits, escapists who flee the world. They are practitioners of a kind of thoroughly individualistic freedom. Later the Chinese Zen school called them "board bearers" or "those who only understand themselves." The expression "board bearer" refers to someone who walks along carrying a board across his shoulder and is able to see only on one side.

CHAPTER 5

Mahayana Thought

Chinese Buddhism has always included and practiced both Mahayana and Hinayana together, and integrated the exoteric and esoteric teachings harmoniously. Even if it views the Hinayana from the Mahayana point of view as not being the ultimate Buddha Dharma at all, nevertheless learning the Mahayana still requires the three Hinayana studies of discipline, meditation, and insight as a foundation. Not only that; if we speak in terms of vehicles or ways, Chinese Buddhism has stages equivalent to five vehicles.

The first is the human vehicle. The study of Buddhism first must begin with being human. Everything that demands careful attention in terms of human social virtues must be accomplished to arrive at doing good and getting rid of evil, thus to abide in the state of perfect goodness. By way of sublimation through the human vehicle, it is then possible to arrive at the more advanced practice of the second vehicle, which is the celestial vehicle; the celestial human is born from perfect goodness in being human.

Third is the *sravaka* vehicle of the Hinayana, which consists of Hinayana practitioners who detach from the world and learn to cultivate practical application of the four truths of suffering, accumulation, extinction, and the path. Beyond this is the fourth vehicle, that of *pratyeka-buddhas*. These are Hinayana practitioners who observe the conglomeration and dissolution of the conditions of the world. When they can observe through meditation accomplishment the arising of conditions and the perishing of conditions, in accord with the principle of the twelve causal conditions, they can abandon the world to stand alone transcendentally beyond things.

The fifth vehicle is finally the path of the bodhisattvas of the Mahayana. "Bodhisattva" is a Sanskrit word composed of the roots *bodhi* (enlightenment) and *sattva* (sentient being). It includes the meanings of self-help and helping others, as well as the meanings of self-enlightenment, enlightenment of others, and complete fulfillment of awareness and action proper to the fruit of Buddhahood. When the term is expressed through direct Chinese translation of the meaning, "bodhisattva" is rendered as "enlightened being," or "great being," or "awakened being." In modern terms, a bodhisattva is a sympathetic illuminate possessed of a kindness and compassion devoted to saving the world. Later Chinese literature contains the expression, "nonmundanity is the skeleton of immortality; sympathy is the heart of Buddhahood." This is really an appropriate picture, beautifully expressed.

The Mahayana bodhisattva path also has three

kinds of courses. The first course is to initially seek one's own benefit, such as beginning with Hinayana transmundane practice, before setting out to save others. In this course, only after one's own salvation is complete does one devote oneself fully to helping others. The second course is first seeking to help others before seeking to liberate oneself. The third is to pursue the course of trying to simultaneously help oneself and others as well.

In sum, the conduct of the Mahayana involves being physically in the world while mentally beyond the world; it is founded on helping society and saving sentient beings, and can be regarded as sacrificing one's own self for the salvation of the world and humanity. The Mahayana view of all sentient beings is to regard them as all of the same body as oneself, thus producing the power of vows of kindness and compassion. The Mahayana kindness and compassion in helping beings are unconditional and make no demands; they are absolutely altruistic attitudes that are produced by oneself and awakened by oneself. Summing up these two ideas, they are called "empathic kindness and unconditional compassion."

The Mahayana system of thought fully extends the Hinayana teachings of discipline, concentration, insight, liberation, and liberated knowledge and insight, to form the stages known as the six ways of transcendence (six *paramitas*) or the ten ways of transcendence.

The first of the so-called six ways of transcendence is giving. Mahayana thought starts here because all sentient beings create suffering as a result of egotistic and selfish craving. In the Mahayana, all that belongs and pertains to the ego is used to make charitable gifts to satisfy the desires of sentient beings, so as to influence and transform their stinginess and greed.

Giving is divided into three types. The first type is the giving of externals: here, making gifts of material goods, physical life, and so on, is called material giving while making gifts of knowledge, learning, and wisdom is called giving of teaching. The second type is internal giving, which is to make one's own inner mind relinquish all greedy and covetous attitudes. The third type is giving of fearlessness, which means to give all sentient beings peace, security, freedom from fear, spiritual support, and assurance.

The second way of transcendence is discipline, beginning with not killing, not stealing, not abusing sexuality, and not telling lies, and extending to the motivations that arouse the mind, all of which are to be regulated by discipline. The Mahayana rules of discipline are not just rules of conduct and appearance; in reality, they are mental precepts intended to govern the mind completely. For example, if the motive for doing good is to gain a reputation, this is considered in violation of the Mahayana bodhisattva precepts. The subtlety of application is truly such that it cannot be exhausted in a few words.

The third way of transcendence is tolerance. To explain the overall essentials simply according to the Mahayana, two expressions can be used to sum up the "Tolerate what others cannot tolerate, carry out what others cannot carry out." The whole thing starts out from the intention to save the world with kindness and compassion, yet it is necessary to reach the point at which one does not have any idea of tolerance in the inner mind; only then does it count as tolerance.

The fourth way of transcendence is diligence. This means diligently arousing a constant determination, at all times and in all places, to exert effort to seek realization.

Therefore, diligence is a companion of the foregoing giving, discipline, and tolerance, as well as of the subsequent meditation and wisdom. Whatever the way of transcendence one is working on, unflagging diligence is necessary. It is a matter of actively doing good, not passively waiting for goodness.

The fifth way of transcendence is meditation concentration. This includes the contents of the four meditations, eight concentrations, and nine successive stages of concentration, fully extending them to where one is in a state of meditation concentration at all times and in all places, in movement and stillness, inside and outside. Even if one ascends to heaven and experiences bliss there, or descends into hell to liberate sentient beings, in all events it is imperative to master oneself by not leaving meditation concentration for so much as a single instant.

The sixth way of transcendence is *prajna*. *Prajna* is a Sanskrit word that is translated into Chinese as "wisdom." However, the Chinese word "wisdom" is often associated with intelligence; in Buddhism, intelligence is called "worldly knowledge and discursive intelligence," which comes from keenness of the sense organs, clarity and brilliance of ears and eyes, none of which is adequate to represent the inner wisdom of *prajna*.

The wisdom of *prajna* contains five meanings. One is the *prajna* of the character of reality, which is realization of knowledge of the fundamental substance of the life of myriad beings in the cosmos and the root source of the essence of mind. Second is the *prajna* of states, which comes from the different states produced by the basic capacity of the essence of mind, and includes the various phenomena of the spiritual world. Third is the *prajna* of words, which is literary and linguistic genius deriving from the philosophy produced by wisdom. Fourth is the *prajna* of expedient means, referring to the methods of applying wisdom, including the domain of learned knowledge. Fifth is auxiliary *prajna*, which is the totality of the virtue deriving from the preceding five ways of transcendence.

The first five ways of transcendence, from giving to meditation, are all bases of the virtues of the intensive Mahayana practice of perfect goodness. By diligent practice of goodness and virtue until one opens up the door by oneself, one arrives at the ultimate fruit of achieving *prajna* wisdom. Therefore, in the highest attainments of both Mahayana and Hinayana Buddhism, emphasis is placed on the liberation of wisdom and the perfection of wisdom; neither depend on blind faith.

By extension of the fulfillment of the six ways of transcendence, making them into means of entering the world to help society and help people, there come to be four additional ways of transcendence. The seventh way of transcendence is skill in means, which are methods of promoting self-help and help for others. The eighth way of transcendence is vowing, which is the eternal infinite power of vows of kindness and compassion for all sentient beings. Therefore, Mahayana bodhisattvas make vows to save the world, with firm promises as expressed by the famous sayings, "Space may have an end, but my vows will have no end," and "As long as hell is not emptied, I promise not to become a Buddha."

The ninth way of transcendence is power, which means producing the great power of determination to help oneself and help others by firm and unshakably faithful commitment. The tenth way of transcendence is knowledge, the great knowledge by which one ultimately arrives at "self enlightenment and enlightenment of others, awareness and action completely fulfilled," and attains the fruit of Buddhahood.

Mahayana Practice

The philosophy of the Mahayana bodhisattva path opens up the Hinayana philosophy of detachment from the world, transforming it into a spirit of active entry into the world. It aims not only to use the transmundane mentality to leap into the fiery hell of the human realm to save the world and save people; it also aims to save all sentient beings. It does not aim to liberate and transform only good people, but also aims to liberate and transform monsters as well. It does not laud only good men and women who sincerely believe in the truth of the Buddha Way; it also lauds other religions and different paths that have this same truth and same principle: Even if they have formulated dissimilar methods and styles of teaching because of differences in their highest visions, as long as they have at heart this same kindness and compassion and awakening of the world, they are recognized as worthy companions engaged in the same activity, the same as the Mahayana bodhisattva path.

This sort of transmundane mentality that does not contend with the world, this completely unconditional, spontaneous commitment to enter the world to save sentient beings, is just like the symbol of the lotus blossom used in later Buddhism. The lotus is a flower of sacred purity that is completely clean and undefiled; but it does not grow on high plateaus or mountain summits: it must be where it is dirty and muddy to bloom and produce fruit.

It is because of this that whenever there is talk about the rules of discipline practiced in the Mahayana, it is always said that there are eighty-four thousand of them, using this expression to describe their manifold details. But this is not a fixed number, it just illustrates the different changing forms of good and bad psychological patterns in the realm of sentient beings: in the space of a single thought, there are eighty-four thousand different ways of slipping.

Thus it is obvious that the fundamental spirit of what we call the disciplinary rules of the Mahayana is in the discipline of mind. In general, it is "correcting your nature whenever you stir your mind." The inner motives within the arousing of intent and stirring of thought immediately break the bodhisattva rules of discipline if they include any bad thoughts at all, or if they emerge from selfishness and self-serving.

Since the T'ang and Sung dynasties, the bodhisattva precepts used in China proper are based on the *Brahmajala sutra;* whereas those used in the borderlands and Tibetan regions are based on the bodhisattva precepts of the *Yogacarya shastra.* However, with both of these books of precepts, the principles and rules and the subtleties of their application are still of one mind.

Most of the principles contained therein are the same as the way of the sage, the wise, and the exemplary as taught in Confucianism, and the conduct proper to people imbued with the Tao. If you read them together with corresponding parts of the *Book of Rites,* which is among the five classics of traditional Chinese culture, you will be able to understand the great work Shakyamuni Buddha did for human morals and mores. It really evokes serious respect from people and induces implicit faith. Rather than call these the precepts of his religion, it would be preferable to say that they are the highest principles of human educational philosophy.

So we know that the spirit of practice of the Mahayana is far from encompassed within the framework of the precepts of the Hinayana. Therefore, the Buddhism in China since the T'ang and Sung dynasties, with its tendency to take from both Mahayana and Hinayana precepts, placing importance on both together, and especially its preference for the practice of Mahayana precepts, is in these respects quite different from Southern Buddhism.

This also shows that China's past cultural tradition did not take in Buddhism all of a sudden: first it had to go through assessment by the yardsticks of Confucian and Taoist thinking before its value was recognized and accepted. Even so, if we speak in terms of the spirit of self-sacrifice of the Mahayana bodhisattva, elevating the aspirations to the heights of devotion to saving the world, of course this is admired by celestials and humans, and none can repudiate it. But when it comes actually to treading that path, it is easier said than done.

Even the altruism shown by the Chinese sage Mo-tzu in wearing himself out to help the world has already been called excessively idealistic by some people, to say nothing of those who surpass Mo-tzu in being able to give up their heads, eyes, brains, and marrow. Therefore, scholars of later eras who earnestly believed in Confucianism presented a hierarchy of benevolence and love, "be familiar with relatives, be benevolent to the people, be loving to beings," which they considered to be a philosophy for saving the world that was rather closer to human sentiment.

Thus learned disquisitions arose that argued about proprieties of conduct according to Confucianism and Buddhism. But when all is said and done, "a high mountain is looked up to, a great deed is to be undertaken." Even if it is too high to climb or too far to reach, nevertheless take the best example; this too is an imperative requirement for teaching and development.

Usually when people ask me if I am a Buddhist, my answer is that I do not have the qualifications to be a Buddhist. When people ask me how one must be to be worthy of being called a Mahayana bodhisattva, the example I give is this. Suppose you were way out on the ocean and ran into a typhoon, and you were about to drown in the billowing waves; at that moment, suppose you had only one lifesaver. Would you sincerely and respectfully give it to the next person? Suppose you were in a famine, on the brink of death from starvation, and you had one bowl of rice, but you preferred to give it to the next person, who was also starving. If you have this kind of heart, then whether or not you have any faith, or have different faiths, you are all equally on the path of the bodhisattva.

A story in Mahayana Buddhism tells of a filial son who approached a bodhisattva who was practicing the path, and requested that the bodhisattva donate his eye so it could be made into medicine to cure his mother. This bodhisattva gouged out his left eye without any reluctance and gave it to the young man, but the filial son objected, "You were too hasty, and made a mistake; I need your right eye to cure my mother." Hearing this, the bodhisattva hesitated a moment, then gouged out his right eye and handed it over. The filial son then said, "I don't need it; your hesitation and reluctance to give it up have rendered the eye ineffective as a medicine."

Hearing this story, we can understand how difficult it is to sacrifice oneself to help the world and help people in actual practice. Of course, in this world of multitudinous sentient beings, there are quite a few examples of "giving up one's life unbegrudgingly, dying for justice serenely," as well as numerous examples of selfless work for others, in various forms, in various manners, some great, some small. As a matter of fact, everywhere is naturally filled with the spirit of the Mahayana bodhisattvas; you cannot say they are not bodhisattvas because they have no religious faith, or because they have different faiths.

When it comes to their theoretical foundation, the bodhisattva precepts clearly define the tendencies and modes of right and wrong, good and bad, in a most thorough and detailed manner. If this sort of spirit is misused, it is not only of no help to the world and of no benefit either to others or oneself; in extreme cases it can even be counterproductive. That requires a separate discussion.

Mahayana Methods of Seeking Realization

The order of the process of actual practice of the Mahayana bodhisattva path is divided into ten steps, which in Buddhist terminology are called the "ten stages." Before one arrives at the first of these ten stages, one must experience four preliminary phases, which comprise forty different levels. Certainly differentiating the Mahayana path into a process of ten stages essentially lies in expanding the mental capacity for kindness and compassion to attain the ultimate principle of discovering truth and fulfilling nature, with the order of the Mahayana stages determined by matching them with the order of the ten transcendent ways.

But this still belongs to the domain of vision or perception; at the same time we must have meditation and concentration states for actual applied function (mental work and virtuous conduct), so that perception and practice complement each other. Thereby one may hope to attain the fruit of Buddhahood, in which perception and realization are fully complete, and great knowledge and great awareness are consummate. In reality, the methods used for seeking realization by the Hinayana, the four meditations, eight concentrations, and nine successive concentrations, are also methods common to the Mahayana.

To arrive at the ultimate limit of comprehension of human nature and comprehension of the nature of beings and things by fully expanding the mental capacity for kindness and compassion is the attainment of the insight and the enlightenment of the mind of the Mahayana bodhisattva. This belongs to the domain of the virtues of perception. At the same time it is necessary to combine states cultivated and realized by meditation and concentration. This is the Mahayana bodhisattva's actual experience, and belongs to the domain of accomplishment by deliberate effort.

However, it is decadent for a bodhisattva to become addicted to the pleasure of meditation concentration and give up the kind and compassionate mind of enlightenment, or not to seek progress in perception to arrive at the fruition of Buddhahood. In sum, the basic principle of Mahayana practice is to constantly keep to the great commitment to save the world and sentient beings. Its ultimate end is the perfection of great knowledge and wisdom to be in the world, yet beyond the world at the same time, with the mind itself liberated. This is what is meant by the expression "samsara and nirvana are like last night's dream; enlightenment and affliction are like flowers in the sky." Only then is the great work done by which one becomes an impeccable teacher of the celestial and the human.

Beyond this, the main scriptures of the various sections of Mahayana and Hinayana Buddhist learning all use the format of dialogue or records of Buddha's words to explain the truths of human life and the universe in thorough detail. Some start with an examination of body and mind to investigate the ultimate limits of the reality realm (a Buddhist technical term that includes the universe). Some analyze body and mind from the point of view of the inherent nature of the fundamental substance of the reality realm. The aim, however, is always to seek realization of liberation.

From the time of the Sui and T'ang dynasties, Chinese Buddhist schools, including the Esoteric Buddhism of the Tibetan regions, all set up their own system of organization and comparative criticism. Thus Buddhist teachings were analyzed and divided according to the T'ien-t'ai school, the Hua-yen school, and the Esoteric school, producing the systems of Chinese Buddhism. Even though each of these schools studied Buddhism from different points of view, their basic principles and doctrines did not diverge very much.

For example, scriptures such as the *Flower Ornament* and *Complete Enlightenment sutras* explain body and mind on the basis of the fundamental substance of the inherent nature of the reality realm. The *Heroic March sutra* and *Diamond sutra* are among those that trace their way back to the source of the inherent nature of the reality realm by way of introspective examination of body and mind. Scriptures such as the *Lotus of Truth* and *Nirvana sutra* say that mind, Buddha, and sentient beings are not different in essence, but change in a single thought between delusion and enlightenment. Scriptures such as the *Great Sun sutra* and the *Esoteric Vehicle sutra* speak of using the temporal to realize the true, based on the nonduality of reality and illusion.

Subsequently it became a standard custom to make a general distinction, in later Buddhism after the passing of Shakyamuni, between schools of essence expounding emptiness and schools of characteristics expounding existence. The schools of *prajna* and contemplation of the center represent the quintessence of the "ultimate emptiness" of the schools of essence; whereas the schools of Consciousness Only and characteristics of phenomena represent the mainstream of the "existence in the ultimate sense" of the schools of characteristics.

So those who liked simple clarity and disliked analysis followed a combination of the emptiness of *prajna* and the teaching of Zen, and those who liked detailed investigation and esteemed logical thinking followed the Consciousness Only teachings on existence to formulate a magnificent array of Buddhist thought. Not only can these be used to pursue a synthesis with and mutual elucidation of Western philosophy, psychology, logic, and other fields of learning imported in recent times; the trend is very much to want to use the Consciousness Only teachings to accommodate, coordinate, and criticize Western philosophy. But this process and goal are still at an early stage of first steps: the question of how to combine Eastern and Western cultures in the same furnace, to enable them to produce a new vista of light, still awaits the efforts and accomplishments of young students of today and people of tomorrow.

PART III
An Outline of the Zen School

CHAPTER 6

Zen and Its Roots

The Zen school is a combination of the mental reality of Shakyamuni Buddha's teaching with the spirit of Chinese culture, forming Chinese Buddhism, blending the most refined and purified schools of ancient Indian Buddhist philosophy. In Buddhist study, "Zen concentration" is a method of cultivating realization practiced by both Hinayana and Mahayana, the Small Vehicle and the Great Vehicle.

The original term for "Zen concentration" is *dhyana*. This is also translated in Chinese as "quiet meditation." Later, the sound of the Sanskrit word *dhyana* Zen was used in conjunction with "concentration" to translate the meaning, thus forming the term conventionally used in Chinese Buddhism, "Zen concentration" or "meditation concentration."

Although the Zen school is not other than the cultivation and realization of Zen concentration, it is not exactly the same thing as Zen concentration. Therefore, it is also called the Mind school, or the *Prajna* school. "Mind school" indicates that the Zen school is the transmission of the mental reality of Buddhist teachings. *Prajna* refers to the Zen schools from the T'ang dynasty on, which placed emphasis on the scriptures on *prajna* (wisdom) and on seeking realization of the liberation of wisdom. In recent times European scholars have also called it the Bodhidharma school, naming it after the great Indian teacher Bodhidharma, who was the first one to transmit the Zen school to China.

Speaking of the Zen school, ever since World War II, Japanese Buddhists, with the support of their government, have made an effort to disseminate Buddhist culture in Europe and America, with particular emphasis on the Zen sect. Because of this, studies dealing with the Zen sect have become a most fashionable and modish field of scholarship in present-day Europe and America, but the parent country of Zen, which is China, has been forgotten and even disdained. The formation of such phenomena truly causes a sinking heaviness in our feelings that is hard to express in words. Even though the momentum of the times makes it this way, yet is it not a human affair?

But the Zen school as talked about right now in China and elsewhere (including Japan) has been deviating on farther and farther tangents along with the trends of the times. Because of this, some people in foreign countries think movements such as the Hippies were inspired by Zen. From the standpoint of Chinese culture, this is really a very big misunderstanding. Strictly speaking, it is also a stain of dishonor that we Eastern cultures have called down upon ourselves.

In general, there are six large misunderstandings of what is presently called Zen. The first comes from the establishment of the terminology of Zen scholarship. Zen originally emphasizes genuine realization through the activities of body and mind, giving parallel weight to work and insight. Once it changes into Zen scholarship, Zen becomes a kind of learned way of thought and can lose its connection with true realization in action and work. At this point "mouth Zen," the fashion of talking about Zen, becomes popular, creating a regressive historical pattern much like the phenomenon of Occult Conversation (*Hsuan-t'an*) in the Chin dynasty (265–419).

The overlooked facts are as follows. After the Zen school was established around the turn of the Sui and T'ang dynasties (ca. 600), it passed through its most flourishing era in the T'ang and Sung dynasties, then continued through the Yuan and Ming dynasties, ending in the Ch'ing. Over a period of more than a thousand years, in areas encompassing East Asia and the lands of Southeast Asia, the way of the Zen school was very popular. Yet we have information on no more than about two thousand people, and those whose practice of Zen was really complete numbered no more than three or four hundred people. And among these, the great adepts were so few you could count them. When was there ever "Zen at all times, Tao in all places"?

Furthermore, if we set aside the sense of the moment captured in stories of Zen living and Zen dialogue, we are left with the virtuous conduct and work of cultivating realization practiced by true Zennists, which are exemplary and honorable ways of upstanding people. So when were true Zen practitioners ever professional talkers who just spouted empty words, failing to reveal any actual accomplishment in their practice of daily living? But to talk about Zen learning is a little better than burying Zen altogether, so in that sense it's all right.

The second misunderstanding derives from the fondness of Oriental scholars for intellectualizing and philosophizing about the literature of Lao-tzu and Chuang-tzu, due to which they perpetuate the myth that Zen has been influenced by the philosophy of these men, or, to put it another way, that Zen is just Taoistic Buddhism amalgamating the philosophy of Lao-tzu and Chuang-tzu. In reality, although Zen and Buddhism have borrowed many terms and expressions from the technical languages of Lao-Chuang (Taoism) and Confucianism, nevertheless they are just borrowings; the spirit of Zen itself is not by any means to be considered a remake or remodeled form of Lao-Chuang or Taoist thought just because it borrows some of their terms and expressions.

For example, if we were to translate Chinese or Buddhist literature, in any given area we would have to make use of terminology from the religious and philosophical languages of that area. But we could only say that similarities between them make communication possible. We cannot say that the result itself represents the ideas of such and such a religion or philosophy. To give another example, when we use Taiwanese money, in certain situations we represent the figures in terms of U.S. dollar equivalents, but it cannot be said that we use U.S. dollars as our national currency.

The third misunderstanding is picking up situational actions and pivotal words found in the method of transmitting Zen teaching and turning them into a distorted lofty silence or parody, always speaking ambiguously and cryptically, while considering this to be the state of Zen. This misleads people quite a bit.

The fourth misunderstanding is to think that Zen is sitting quietly with a blank mind and closed eyes (what is commonly called just sitting), or that it is deep thought or silent reverie. This is the case of those who follow tangents and byways, and there are many such people who represent things like this as Zen. That is why advertisements for the transmission of various kinds of Zen or meditation work appear in the newspapers, and have become a popular business.

The fifth misunderstanding is found among American youth of recent times who employ hallucinogenic drugs such as LSD in conjunction with unrestrained behavior and various occult ideas, thinking that they are then doing Zen meditation and achieving the effects equivalent to Zen work. Although most countries have outlawed the sale of hallucinogens, they are still available and continue to be used in this fashion. These drugs were originally used in the diagnosis and treatment of mental illness, but when they are diverted from that and associated with Zen, it is really a big joke.

The sixth misunderstanding comes from the popular dissemination of Indian yoga in Europe and America after World War II. The body-strengthening exercises of yoga also place great emphasis on the practice of quiet sitting. Thus, in some cases self-hypnosis has been combined with yogic exercises for cultivating life force energy and developing its circulation, with this being taken for Zen. Fish eyes are mixed with pearls, deer are called horses; thus people who do not understand the ultimate have a hard time making the appropriate distinctions.

Historical Traces of Zen

Within the context of Buddhism, Zen has always been called the teaching that is transmitted separately outside of doctrine. It is traditionally told that when Shakyamuni addressed a crowd of a million people and celestial beings at a meeting on Spiritual Mountain, he remained silent and did not speak a word; he just held up a flower and twirled it, showing it to everyone in the great assembly. No one could comprehend his meaning, except for Maha (Elder) Kasyapa, who smiled in understanding. Then Shakyamuni announced to the crowd, "I have the treasury of the eye of true teaching, the ineffable mind of nirvana. The form of reality is formless; the subtle teaching does not insist on written words, but is separately transmitted outside of doctrine. This I entrust to Maha Kasyapa."

This was the beginning of Zen. Later the reverend Kasyapa was considered the first patriarch of Zen in India, and Ananda was the second patriarch; the patriarchy was handed on through the generations, until it reached the twenty-eighth patriarch, Great Master Bodhidharma. At that time in China, it was the era of the Northern and Southern dynasties, and Indian Buddhism was in decline. Bodhidharma thought that China had the atmosphere of the Mahayana, so he crossed the sea to come East. Arriving in Canton province, he met with Emperor Wu of the Liang dynasty in southern China.

Emperor Wu was a devoted believer in religion; he not only believed in Buddhism but he honored Taoism as well. So when he saw the Great Master Bodhidharma, he immediately asked, "I have constructed so many temples and performed so many Buddhist services; how much merit do you think I have earned?"

Now it happened that Bodhidharma was transmitting the seal of the Buddha mind and was carrying out a mission to disseminate the mental teaching of true Buddhism, so he answered frankly, "No merit whatsoever. These are just minor effects on the human or celestial levels, with contaminated causes; like shadows following forms, though they exist, they are not real." He also said, "Pure knowledge is ineffably perfect, inherently empty, and silent; such merit is not sought through the world."

Because the conversation of the emperor and the Zen patriarch did not reach accord, the Great Master crossed over into northern China, where he stayed at Shao-lin temple on Mount Sung and sat facing a wall. Since he spent his days in silence, no one could fathom him. Later he transmitted the mind teaching, together with the robe and bowl symbolic of the succession, to the second Zen patriarch of China, Shen-kuang. This is the *kung-an*, or public record, of Great Master Bodhidharma coming East to become the first patriarch of Chinese Zen.

Ever since the T'ang and Sung dynasties, some scholars researching Buddhist doctrines and principles have verbosely criticized the Zen history of the raising of the flower and the smile and the special transmission outside of doctrine, without themselves having attained any understanding whatsoever of the Zen teachings on practice and realization, and in extreme cases having their own biased attitudes. Even down to the present day there are still people who do not believe this story, and who even entertain doubts about Great Master Bodhidharma's transmission of the teaching; they take these to be the fabrications of Chinese monks. They actually believe that the

Zen school was a revolutionary party within Chinese Buddhism, and that it was single-handedly invented in the T'ang dynasty by Shen-hui (also called Ho-tse), a minor disciple of the sixth patriarch Hui-neng.

Since people have already raised these problems, we might as well provide some explanation. If such ideas are rooted in an attitude of love for the tradition of Chinese culture, recognizing fine scholarship as a product of Chinese people and thus denying the traditional explanation of the transmission of Zen, that is understandable. But if they are based on an attitude of opposition to tradition and custom, on a habitual fondness for going against the norm regardless, on any issue at all to give the appearance of lofty purism, that is out of harmony with the principle of "learning a lot, leaving aside the doubtful, and speaking carefully of the rest."

Actually, concerning doubts about the source material on the Zen history of the special transmission outside of doctrine, Wang An-shih of the Sung dynasty did present proof that there was such a thing; but the authentication has already been lost, and it was not very strong evidence anyway. Nevertheless, if you read through the Buddhist scriptures, you can find a number of indirect proofs; but since this would take too long and be too specialized, I will refrain from going into them here. In sum, whenever dealing with facts or doing scholarship, "see a lot, set aside the doubtful, and practice the rest with care." But the attitude of conscious doubt, bringing up questions to seek answers, is the most enlightened way of dealing with things, as long as it is not done too subjectively.

As for the spirit of the initial transmission of Zen to China, when Great Master Bodhidharma was sitting silently facing a wall at Shao-lin temple, someone asked him why he had come to China. His reply was that he was looking for someone who "was not influenced by the deceptions of others." The meaning of this statement is most profound; try to think of who can reach the point of being completely immune to being deceived by anyone of any time or place? Indeed, we are all sometimes involved in our own self-deception. If an individual can really reach the point of being immune to all deception, even if that person does not become a sage or a Buddha, he or she is still an extraordinary human being. Generally, only people who are immovable because they are either of the highest wisdom or the lowest ignorance can achieve this!

A certain young man from Lo-yang named Chi Kuang had read widely in the classics and was particularly well versed in Lao-tzu and Chuang-tzu. But he used to say with regret that the teachings of Confucius and Lao-tzu only established human cultural rites and doctrines, and guides for worldly learning. Furthermore, he felt that the books of Chuang-tzu and the *I Ching,* although mysterious and profound, were still unable to exhaust thoroughly the marvelous principles of the universe and human life. Because of this he eventually gave up worldly learning and left home to become a monk, changing his name to Shen-kuang.

After this he made a thorough study of the Mahayana and Hinayana Buddhist doctrines. When he reached the age of thirty-three, he went to Mount Hsiang, where he sat quietly all day long for eight years. After that he went to Shao-lin temple to see the Great Master Bodhidharma in search of the Way. At this time, however, the Great Master was constantly sitting facing a wall, and did not give out any instructions at all.

Now Shen-kuang thought to himself, "When people of old sought the Way, they broke open their bones to take out the marrow and pierced their flesh to draw blood in order to feed the hungry, spread their hair over mud for others to walk on, and threw themselves over cliffs to feed tigers. They did this even in ancient times, when human hearts were pure and unspoiled; so what am I worth?" Now it happened to be a snowy winter, yet Shen-kuang stood all night in attendance by the side of Great Master Bodhidharma; by dawn the snow on the ground had piled up so high it passed his knees, yet he kept standing there with even greater reverence. (Later stories of standing in snow at the school of the Ch'engs, famous neo-Confucians of the Sung dynasty, are reproductions of this kind of spirit.)

Great Master Bodhidharma turned to him and asked, "You have been standing there in the snow all night; what are you seeking?" Weeping grievously, Shen-kuang pleaded, "I only hope that the Great Master will be so kind and compassionate as to open up the gate of the ambrosial teaching whereby to liberate sentient beings." But Bodhidharma retorted in a scolding tone, "The unexcelled sublime Way of the Buddhas requires countless eons of diligent practice, refining virtuous conduct through the ability to do what is hard to do and endure what is hard to endure. How can you, with so little virtue and wisdom, and with your casual and arrogant attitude, hope to seek and find the true realization of the Way? I am afraid your concern is in vain."

Hearing this upbraiding, Shen-kuang took out a

sharp sword, cut off his own left forearm, and placed it before the Great Master, to show how earnestly determined he was in seeking the Way. Now the Great Master Bodhidharma recognized the young man's capacity to bear great responsibility, and changed his name to Hui-k'e.

Then Shen-kuang asked, "Would you explain to me the teaching of the seal of the mind of all Buddhas?" The Great Master replied, "The truth of the mind of Buddhas is not attained from another!" (Please note that this statement is the most important key of Zen.)

Hearing this, Shen-kuang asked, "My mind is not at ease; please teach me how to pacify the mind." The Great Master then told him, "Find your mind for me, and I will pacify it for you."

Shen-kuang was stupefied when he heard this. After a long while he finally said, "I have searched for where my mind is, but I cannot find it!" Then the Great Master said, "Right! This is how to pacify your mind!" He also taught him a method of practice: "You must set aside all external objects, and make your inner mind free from waves. Still the mind so that it is like a wall, stopping random movements inside and outside, exiting and entering, coming and going. Then you can enter the Way by this means." Later he also instructed him to use the *Lankavatara sutra* to authenticate his own practice and understanding. This is the course of events in the *kung-an,* or public record, of Great Master Bodhidharma first transmitting Zen in China, handing it on to the second patriarch Shen-kuang.

Now, based on these stories of the handing on of the initial transmission of Zen, we will address three separate issues to explain them.

The Special Transmission of Zen Outside of Buddhist Doctrine

The so-called "special transmission" of Zen "outside of doctrine" does not mean that there is a secret or arcane transmission that basically does not need the scriptural teachings of Buddhism. The whole body of principles of Buddhist scriptural teachings is for the purpose of explaining the theory and methods of how to cultivate practice and seek realization. Therefore, people who cling to the principles of the scriptural teachings often turn them into philosophical thought, thereby producing the countereffect of increasing intellectual barriers and divisions. Thus they cannot achieve unity of knowledge and action and realize the effect of practice and vision advancing together simultaneously.

So the special transmission outside of doctrine just represents a variance from the usual method of transmission of Buddhism; it does not refer to a special extraordinary teaching outside of the principles of the Buddhist teachings. Shen-kuang, for example, was a learned and talented young man before he became a monk; after he was ordained, he added to this a mastery of the principles of the teachings of Mahayana and Hinayana Buddhism. As far as intellectual knowledge is concerned, clearly he was extraordinary in the depth, breadth, and fullness of his learning; yet he did not want anything but to find his own mind. So he understood that intellectual scholarship that is full of doubt and the genuine application to the matter of finding real spiritual peace and enlightenment are two different things. Therefore, he abandoned intellectual doctrine and just sought real enlightenment.

When one attains to real enlightenment and arrives

at the actual truth, however, this naturally will merge with the basis of intellectual learning that one has, and one will clearly understand the ultimate principle. This is why the later Zen Master Kuei-shan Ling-yu said, "The noumenal ground of reality does not have a single atom in it, yet the avenues of myriad practices do not reject a single method."

So if we draw a general conceptual conclusion about the doctrines of Buddhist teaching and the source of the Zen specially transmitted outside of doctrine, doctrines teach you how to cultivate practice and realize the effects; the source is how we should cultivate practice to seek realization. The source and the doctrines are different only in terms of the method of guidance; they do not have different purposes.

The Work of Zen

The Zen of the Zen school is not "mouth Zen," laying emphasis on turns of phrase expressing thrusts of wit; Zen is not apart from the work of cultivating realization through meditation concentration to arrive at the ultimate result of attaining sagehood or Buddhahood through clarifying the mind and seeing its essence. In the example of Shen-kuang, before he had seen Great Master Bodhidharma he had already steeped his mind in the *I Ching* and the Taoist teachings of Lao-tzu and Chuang-tzu, and he had also gone through strict training to cultivate the mind. Having sat quietly on Mount Hsiang for eight years, he already had a considerable grounding in the work of meticulous introspection to rectify his nature whenever his mind stirred.

When he saw Bodhidharma, not only did the Great

Master not immediately give Shen-kuang guidance, instead he spurred him on with an unbearable attitude and extreme words. If Shen-kuang had been a man without real cultivation, even if he did not punch Bodhidharma out, at least he would have left at once; but instead he increased his sincerity and seriousness, even to the point where he cut off his arm to seek the Way. Based on this kind of spirit, we might well paraphrase the Confucian Hsia-tzu to say, "Even though it might be said that he had not yet entered the Way, I would call this the Way!" So when he asked Bodhidharma how to pacify the mind, the Great Master just told him, "Bring me your mind and I will pacify it for you." Then he was able to awaken to the Way with the understanding that "having looked for the mind, it cannot be found."

In later eras, people researching Zen have tended to talk about it as sudden enlightenment at a word, immediately attaining Buddhahood, as if it just required intellectual acuity, and as if the ability to utter one or two pretty phrases immediately counted as enlightenment. They have completely disregarded the important points of real learning and real work. Of course their behavior falls into the category of "wild fox Zen" that makes you wonder who they think they are fooling. Do they think they are fooling people? Do they think they are fooling Heaven?

There are also those who think they do not need to work on introspection themselves, but must only find an enlightened teacher to transmit a secret way of opening, imagining that this is the work of Zen. People with this attitude have also forgotten the clear lesson of the Great Master Bodhidharma that "The seal of truth of the Buddhas is not gotten from another." Modern discussions of Zen either fall easily into the vanity of the former view or the occultism of the latter. This is really worth reflecting upon.

Using the *Lankavatara Sutra* to Seal One's Understanding of Penetrating Through to the Root Basis of Mind and the Universe

The Zen initially transmitted by Great Master Bodhidharma was communicated to several students besides the second patriarch Shen-kuang, who personally received the robe and bowl of Bodhidharma and inherited the enlightenment lineage of the Zen school. All of these students had mental attainment, but their talents, virtues, and spirits were somewhat inferior to those of Shen-kuang.

Besides transmitting the mind teaching, at the same time Great Master Bodhidharma still wanted Shen-kuang to seal the mind with the *Lankavatara sutra*. By this we can see that the Zen specially transmitted outside of doctrine is not separate from the principles of the teachings at all. The *Lankavatara sutra* was, after all, handed on to Shen-kuang by Great Master Bodhidharma to be a valuable reference book for sealing the mind. Yet in the Fa-hsiang (Dharmalakshana) or Wei-shih (Vijnaptimatra) school of Mahayana Buddhism, it is also recognized as one of the main classic scriptures of Only Consciousness studies.

The *Lankavatara sutra* presents the method for seeking realization represented by the expression "the door of nonbeing is the door to truth." It also explains how sudden enlightenment and gradual cultivation are both important. At the same time, it divides the substance and function of mental phenomena into eight functions, which consist of the five primary consciousnesses, which are the eye, ear, nose, tongue, and body consciousnesses, plus the sixth or ideational consciousness, the seventh or mental consciousness, and the eighth or storehouse consciousness. This is what is called the analysis of one mind into eight consciousnesses.

Anciently it was noted that consciousness has the functions of discernment and discrimination and also includes the capacities of feeling, cognition, and spiritual activity. The sixth or ideational consciousness is also divided into two levels, a consciousness that comprehends and a consciousness of images alone (also called solitary ideational consciousness). The ideational consciousness of images alone corresponds to what modern psychology calls the phenomenon of the subconscious.

The seventh or mind consciousness is the faculty of the intellect, which is the consciousness of the original cognitive awareness and instinctive activity that come along with self and life. The eighth or storehouse consciousness is the monad that includes both mind and objects, the basis of the nature of mind, which is at the root of both the spiritual world and the material world.

Thus we can see that the clarification of mind and perception of its essence as spoken of in Zen does not simply mean psychological peace of mind. In reality it requires us to penetrate through the root basis of the universe, body, and mind. Only then can we really know the truth of the statement that "the three realms are only mind, myriad phenomena are only consciousness."

The overall gist of the *Lankavatara sutra* brings into play the general outline of Only Consciousness studies, which consists of the following: five phenomena (names, appearances, discrimination, accurate knowledge, suchness as is); three inherent natures (relative, merely conceptual, perfectly real); eight consciousnesses (as explained above); and two kinds of selflessness (of person, of things). In sum, the doctrinal principles of the *Lankavatara sutra* lay greatest emphasis on analytic observation and insight, entering minutely into where there is no gap, penetrating completely through the substance and function of the nature of mind.

The method of Zen is to absorb the principles and concentrate on single-minded cultivation of realization in harmony with the principles of the teachings. Therefore, in later Zen there was a famous proverb that said, "If you master the source but not the teachings, whenever you open your mouth you will speak at random; if you master the teachings but not the source, you will be like a one-eyed dragon." In reality, this idea is just a rephrasing of the expressions used in the *Lankavatara sutra* itself referring to mastery of the source and mastery of the explanation.

Recently some people have presented the Zen school before the sixth patriarch under the rubric of the Lankavatara school, and have thereby treated Zen after the sixth patriarch as a separate domain. Actually, this is a result of not understanding the real Zen mind teaching. They did not avoid adding legs to a drawing of a snake, making an unnecessary step.

When Great Master Bodhidharma was entrusting the transmission to the second patriarch Shen-kuang, he predicted, "Two hundred years after my death . . . those who understand the Way will be many, but those who travel the Way will be few. Those who talk about the principle will be many, but those who master the principle will be few."

The doctrine of the *Lankavatara sutra* has thus been turned into a subject of literary and formal scholarship, and has come to be known as nothing but theoretical ideology. This is most lamentable! What is more, some people cite the *Lankavatara sutra's* passage on gradual cultivation as a proof that what Great Master Bodhidharma transmitted was gradual practice Zen, paying no attention to a later passage on the equal importance of the sudden and the gradual. This is really the epitome of crudity and shallowness.

CHAPTER 7

Influences on the Development of Zen Before the Early T'ang Dynasty

From the time Great Master Bodhidharma came East over the sea during the era of Emperor Wu of the Southern Liang dynasty, he remained in China for about twenty years. Aside from his transmission of the Zen mind teaching to the young monk Shenkuang, who became the second patriarch of Zen, he also had a number of other disciples who studied with him at the same time. These were Tao-fu, Tao-yu, the nun Tsungchih, and Yang Hsuan, governor of Ch'i-ch'eng.

Although these disciples did not directly continue the lineage of Zen, they nevertheless took up the very same message of breaking through appearances and detaching from objects, directly pointing to the human mind to see its essence and attain Buddhahood. They naturally developed and spread the work of Zen teaching at the same time, so during the interval between the Southern dynasties of Liang and Ch'en and the Sui dynasty they in turn influenced the Zen meditation of Zen Master Hui-ssu of Nan-yueh, who earnestly cultivated practice of the *Lotus sutra* and *pratyutpanna-samadhi,* concentration on the immediate presence of the Buddhas.

Through this influence, Hui-ssu preached the Zen of direct pointing to mind, saying he was "pointing to things to communicate the mind, but nobody understands." Later his disciple Zen Master Chih-che (Chih-i), who received his robe and bowl, founded the practical teachings of the T'ien-t'ai school, consisting of three kinds of cessation and three kinds of contemplation, thus setting up the first distinct school of Chinese Buddhism after the Dharma Master Hui-yuan had established the Pure Land school during the Chin dynasty.

Chih-i took the methods of meditation concentration practiced in Hinayana Buddhism, combined them with thorough reflection and insightful contemplation of the principles of Mahayana Buddhism, and picked up on the essential points of Zen, which directly points to the human mind to see its essence and attain Buddhahood. Chih-i formed a comprehensive system, making a complete arrangement of the theories of Buddhism, and founded a mode of teaching of real gradual practice in a systematic course of cultivation and realization.

Thus it was that from the end of the Ch'en dynasty and beginning of the Sui dynasty, on through the T'ang, Sung, Yuan, Ming, and Ch'ing dynasties, over a period of more than a thousand years, the grandees of the intelligentsia, the literati, people who liked metaphysics and yet were unwilling to give up the world and their fondness for scholarship, all followed the practical methods of Zen concentration according to the cessation and contemplation exercises of the T'ien-t'ai school. There were also those who combined this with the Zen school: people such as the famous T'ang dynasty gentleman Li Hsiao, who was an outstanding T'ien-t'ai scholar; and others such as Po Chu-i, Lu Fang-weng, Su Tung-p'o, Wang Anshih, and the great neo-Confucians of the early Sung dynasty, all of whom went through a course of T'ien-t'ai cessation and contemplation practice, which is a form of meditation concentration. The meditation concentration first learned by the famous Ming dynasty Confucian Wang Yang-ming was also the T'ien-t'ai cessation and contemplation practice. The famous Ch'ing dynasty scholar Kung Ting-an not only wrote an essay extolling T'ien-t'ai cessation and contemplation meditation concentration; he even made every effort to repudiate the errors of the Zen school.

It is important that this issue be brought to the attention of those who are studying the history of Chinese culture and philosophy, in order that everyone be able to distinguish rigorously the differences between cessation and contemplation meditation concentration and the mind teaching of the Zen school, and to understand the key to the controversy between gradual practice and sudden enlightenment. It is important to understand these issues in the context of the influence of Zen on Chinese philosophy during and after the Sui and T'ang dynasties, as well as the connection between the T'ien-t'ai school and secular scholars over the ages.

In the past, the usual run of professors and Confucianists studying Chinese Buddhism or philosophy felt threatened by the multiplicity and vast scope of the ideas found in Chinese Buddhist studies and the schools of Chinese Buddhism. At a loss to know where to turn, they set about their research in a confused manner and made a central issue of the T'ang dynasty controversy between Southern subitist (sudden) Zen and Northern gradualist Zen. Clearly, they have suffered from bias and confusion.

In reality, from the Sui and T'ang dynasties, through the first century or so of the early T'ang, after Shen-kuang and aside from the five generations of patriarchs who solely transmitted the lineage of the Zen school, there were three other people who studied under Great Master Bodhidharma along with Shen-kuang. While Shen-kuang's formal transmission of the patriarchy went to third Zen patriarch Seng-ts'an, altogether there were seventeen other known great masters over six generations who also belonged to the Shen-kuang succession but were descended from his other disciples who were contemporaries of the third patriarch. The fourth patriarch, Zen Master Tao-hsin, produced one hundred and eighty-three worthies in addition to the fifth patriarch Hung-jen. The famous sixth patriarch Hui-neng was not Hung-jen's only student either, for he had a hundred and seven notable contemporaries who belonged to the succession of Zen Master Hung-jen.

By the time of the fifth Zen patriarch in the early T'ang dynasty, those among these descendants of the Zen patriarchs who were comparatively well known and who can be traced through existing historical source materials, had scattered in the four directions, each setting up paths of guidance, influencing both urban and rural society as well as T'ang dynasty Chinese Buddhism. The establishment of the Hua-yen school also had some connection to the dissemination of the Zen school.

From the time of the reign of empress Wu Tse-t'ien (684–705), there were quite a few disciples in the succession of Zen Master Shen-hsiu of the so-called Northern school. Although the Zen of the Southern school following the sixth patriarch Hui-neng is referred to as the true lineage of the Zen school, this is merely a question of the heritage of succession of the Zen lineage and cannot be taken as an absolute basis for assessing the influence of Zen on the intellectual trends of Chinese culture and philosophy during the T'ang dynasty. Because of this, it seems to me that if one wants to talk about Zen studies, it is first necessary to study Zen truly and correctly, in terms of doing real work in Zen meditation and insight. Only afterwards can one talk about Zen. If one wants to talk about the intellectual history of Zen, or the history of Chinese philosophy and Chinese Buddhism, it is imperative to understand the whole picture; it will not do to generalize about the whole based on a part, or to speak based on a fixation on only one element.

CHAPTER 8

The Sixth Patriarch of Zen

The stories about Master Hui-neng, the sixth patriarch of Chinese Zen, are favorite topics for discussion among people who lecture on Zen and the history of Chinese philosophical thought. I will present a brief introduction to his tale and then discuss several misunderstood issues therein.

Great Master Hui-neng was surnamed Lu in lay life. His ancestors were from Fan-yang (in Hopei, north China), but during the Wu-te era of the reign of Emperor Kao-tsu of the T'ang dynasty (618-626) his father was assigned to a post in Kuang-tung (Canton) province. At the age of three he lost his father, and his mother resolutely took care of him alone until he grew up.

Hui-neng's family was poor and gathered wood for a living. One day as Hui-neng was carrying a load of kindling to market, he happened to hear someone reciting the *Diamond sutra*. When the recitation reached the passage that says, "One should enliven the mind without dwelling on anything," Hui-neng attained a degree of realization. The man who was reciting the sutra told him that it was a Buddhist scripture that the fifth patriarch of Zen, Hung-jen, who was teaching in Huang-mei (Hupei), always instructed people to read. Hui-neng then contrived a way to go to Huang-mei to seek to learn to practice Zen. (At that time he had not yet left society to become a monk.)

When the fifth patriarch, Zen Master Hung-jen, first saw him, he asked, "Where do you come from?"

Hui-neng answered, "From Ling-nan."

The fifth patriarch then asked, "What do you want?"

"I only seek to become a Buddha."

"People from Ling-nan have no Buddha nature; how can you become a Buddha?"

Hui-neng said in reply, "People may be from the south or the north, but how could the Buddha nature have any east or west?"

Hearing this, the fifth patriarch told Hui-neng to go to work with the rest of the people there. The future patriarch said, "My own mind always produces wisdom. Not straying from one's own nature is itself a field of blessings. What would you have me do?" The fifth patriarch saw that his basic nature was extremely sharp, and told him to go pound rice in the mill, so Hui-neng went and labored there for eight months.

Then one day the fifth patriarch announced that he was going to hand on his robe and bowl and would choose someone to inherit the rank of patriarch. Therefore, he told everyone to present an expression of their mental attainment. Now at this time there were over seven hundred monks learning Zen from the fifth patri-arch. Among them was a chief elder named Shen-hsiu, who had thoroughly studied both Buddhist and non-Buddhist classics and was looked up to by everyone in the community for his learning. He knew everyone was counting on him, so he wrote a verse on the wall of the hallway, saying,

> *The body is the tree of enlightenment,*
> *The mind is like a clear mirror on a stand.*
> *Diligently wipe it off again and again,*
> *Don't let it gather dust.*

When the fifth patriarch had seen this verse, he said, "If people of later generations cultivate practice in accord with this, they will also attain superior results." But when Hui-neng heard this verse from the other students, he commented, "That's fine, all right, but not perfect." The other students laughed at him saying, "What does an ordinary man like you know? Don't talk crazy."

Hui-neng replied, "You don't believe me? I would like to add a verse." The other students looked at each other and laughed without giving a reply. That night, Hui-neng secretly summoned a servant boy to come with him to the hall, and asked him to write a verse on the wall next to the one written by Shen-hsiu:

> *Enlightenment basically has no tree,*
> *And the clear mirror has no stand;*
> *Originally there is not a single thing;*
> *Where can dust gather?*

When the fifth patriarch saw this verse, he said, "Who composed this? He has not seen the essence either." Everyone heard what the patriarch said, so they didn't pay the verse any mind. That night, however, the fifth patriarch surreptitiously went to the mill and asked Hui-neng, "Is the rice whitened yet?"

Hui-neng answered, "It is whitened, but has not had a sifting yet." (The word for "sifting" has the same sound as the word for "teacher." This dialogue between teacher and student has a double meaning throughout.)

The fifth patriarch then knocked the pestle three times with his staff, and so Hui-neng entered his room in the third watch of the night, where he received the mental transmission of the fifth patriarch.

At that time the fifth patriarch repeatedly examined Hui-neng's initial understanding of the meaning of "one should enliven the mind without dwelling on anything," whereupon he penetrated all the way through to great enlightenment on hearing the patriarch's words.

Then Hui-neng said, "All things are not apart from our intrinsic nature. Who would have expected that our intrinsic nature is inherently pure? Who would have expected that our intrinsic nature is basically unborn and unperishing? Who would have expected that our intrinsic nature is fundamentally complete in itself? Who would have expected that our intrinsic nature is basically immovable? Who would have expected that our intrinsic nature can produce all things?"

The fifth patriarch answered, "If you do not know the fundamental mind, study of doctrine is useless. If you do know the fundamental mind and see your own basic nature, then you are called a great man, a teacher of celestials and humans, a Buddha." Then he handed on the robe and bowl, making Hui-neng the sixth patriarch of the spiritual lineage of Chinese Zen.

After the fifth patriarch, Hung-jen, had transmitted

the mind seal, that very night he saw the sixth patriarch Hui-neng off on his way across the river to go south. Personally picking up the oar, he said, "I am ferrying you across!" But the sixth patriarch replied, "When deluded, one is 'ferried across' by a guide; when enlightened, one ferries oneself across. Although the expression 'crossing over' is the same, the usage is different. I have received the teacher's communication of the Dharma, and have now attained enlightenment; it is only appropriate that I cross over by myself, of my own nature." Hearing this, the fifth patriarch acceded, "So it is, so it is! Hereafter the Buddha Dharma will flourish through you."

After this, the fifth patriarch stopped giving lectures. The whole community wondered about this, and asked about it, to which the fifth patriarch replied, "My Way has gone! Why inquire after it anymore?" Therefore the students asked, "Who got the robe and the Dharma?" The fifth patriarch replied, "The able one got them."

Now the community got together to discuss this. Since the worker Lu was named (Hui-)*neng,* which means "able," they decided that he must have received the Dharma and slipped away in secret. Therefore, they agreed to pursue him. After two months of searching, one of the party in pursuit, a former military leader who had left society to become a monk, a man named Hui-ming, went ahead and caught up with the sixth patriarch just as he reached the Ta-yu Range.

The sixth patriarch took the robe and bowl and tossed them onto a rock and said, "This robe just symbolizes evidence of truthfulness, that is all; why fight over it?" Hui-ming then tried to pick up the robe and bowl, but found that he could not even move them. He said, "I came for the Dharma, not for the robe!" The sixth patriarch responded, "Since you came for the Dharma, you should stop all entanglements and not give rise to a single thought; then I will explain it for you."

Hearing this, Hui-ming stood still for a very long time; then the sixth patriarch finally said, "Don't think of good, don't think of evil: at this very moment, what is your original face?" Hui-ming attained great enlightenment at these words. He also asked, "Is there any other secret message aside from the esoteric meaning of the esoteric words you have just spoken?" The sixth patriarch said, "What I have told you is not a secret. If you look into yourself, you will find the secret is in you."

Hui-ming then climbed down the mountain and claimed he had found no trace of anyone up on the ridge, and induced the posse to disperse.

After this, the sixth patriarch lived in anonymity among a group of hunters in south China. It was not until fifteen years later that he finally emerged from hiding and went to Fa-hsing monastery in Canton province, where the priest Yin-tsung happened to be lecturing on the *Nirvana sutra*. There he took shelter under the eaves.

One evening, as the wind was causing the monastery banner to flap noisily, two monks were debating about it: one said that it was the banner moving, the other said it was the wind moving. They kept on arguing ceaselessly, so the sixth patriarch commented, "It is not the wind moving, and it is not the banner moving either; it is your minds moving." Because of this he was recognized by the priest Yin-tsung, who announced that he had found the sixth patriarch of Zen. Gathering the whole community, the priest shaved Hui-neng's head, invested him with the precepts, and ordained him as a monk. Subsequently, he lived at Ts'ao-ch'i and spread the Way of Zen widely.

This is a brief history of the enlightenment and teaching of the sixth patriarch of Zen. Based on this story, I will present three issues for study, to enable everyone to avoid further misinterpretations in the understanding of Zen studies and in the investigation of Chinese cultural and philosophical history.

The First Issue

The first issue has to do with the sixth patriarch's enlightenment, clarifying the mind and seeing its essential nature, along with two expressions in Shen-hsiu's verse. In the *Altar Sutra of the Sixth Patriarch,* which has come down through history in several different versions, as well as in the records of the various texts of the Zen school, there are stories about the sixth patriarch's first enlightenment that are not very much different from one another. In Chinese Zen, beginning with the fifth patriarch Hung-jen, people were instructed to recite the *Diamond Prajnaparamita sutra* as a means of entering the Way, thus changing Great Master Bodhidharma's didactic method of using the *Lankavatara sutra* to seal the mind. This can only be called a change in the method of instruction; there is no difference at all in the essential message of Zen. The main import of the *Diamond sutra* is to clarify the mind and see its essential nature. Here and there it explains the truth of essential emptiness as realized by *prajna.* The method of cultivating practice to seek realization therein emphasizes the three words "skillfully guarding mindfulness." It explains the real character of essential emptiness, saying, "the past mind cannot be apprehended, the future mind cannot be apprehended, the present mind cannot be apprehended." The goal is perfect knowledge of "enlivening the mind without dwelling on anything."

For the sake of obtaining a general understanding of the Zen principle of governing the mind, I will presently use modern concepts to make a comparatively easy and lucid explanation. This can also serve as an instructional basis for cultivating practice, because it is a simple and swift method of cultivating mind and nurturing its essential nature.

Step One

First we have to quietly and calmly observe and examine our own inner consciousness and thoughts, and then make a simple analysis in two parts. The first part consists of the thoughts and ideas produced from sensory feelings like pain, pleasure, fullness and warmth, hunger, cold, and so on. All of these belong to the domain of sensory awareness; from them are derived activities of cognitive awareness, such as association and imagination. The other part consists of consciousness and thought produced by cognitive awareness, such as vague emotions, anxieties, anguish, discriminating thoughts regarding people, oneself, and inner or outer phenomena, and so on. Of course the latter part also includes intellectual and scholastic thinking, as well as the very capacity one has to observe one's own psychological functions.

Step Two

The next step comes when you have arrived at the point where you are well able to understand the activity of your own psychological functions.

Whether they be in the domain of sensory awareness or in the domain of cognitive awareness, they
are each referred to generally as a single thought:
when you can reach the point where in the interval
of each thought you can clearly observe each idea
or thought that occurs to your mind, without any
further absentmindedness, unawareness, or vague-
ness, then you can process them into three levels of
observation.

Generally speaking, the preceding thought
(thinking consciousness) that has just passed is
called the past mind, or the prior thought; the suc-
ceeding thought (thinking consciousness) that has
just arrived is called the present mind, or the immediate thought; while that which has yet to come is
of course the future mind, or the latter thought.
However, since the latter thought has not yet come,
you do not concern yourself with it. But you must
not forget that when you take note that the latter
thought has not yet come, this itself is the present
immediate thought; and the moment you realize it
is present, it has at once already become the past.

Step Three
Now the next step is when you have practiced
this inner observation successfully for a long time.
You watch the past mind, present mind, and future
mind with lucid clarity and then develop familiarity
with the state of mind of the immediate present,
when the past mind of the former thought has
gone, and the future mind of the latter thought has
not yet come. This state of mind in the instant of
the immediate present then should subtly and gradually present an open blankness.

But this open blankness is not stupor, lightheadedness, or like the state before death. It is an open awareness that is lucid and clear, numinous and luminous. This is what the Zen masters of the Sung and Ming dynasties used to call the time of radiant awareness.

If you can really arrive at this state, you will then feel that your own consciousness and thinking, whether in the domain of sensory awareness or in the domain of cognitive awareness, are all like reflections on flowing water, like geese going through the endless sky, like the breeze coming over the surface of water, like flying swans over the snow: no tracks or traces can be found. Then you will finally realize that everything you think and do in everyday life is all nothing more than floating dust or reflections of light; there is fundamentally no way to grasp it, fundamentally no basis to rely upon. Then you will attain experiential understanding of the psychological state in which "the past mind cannot be apprehended, the future mind cannot be apprehended, the present mind cannot be apprehended."

Step Four

Next after that, if you really understand the ungraspability of the past, present, and future mind and thought, when you look into yourself it will turn into a laugh.

By this means you will recognize that everything and every activity in this mind is all the ordinary person disturbing himself. From here, take another step further to examine and break through the pressure produced by biological sensation and the physical action and movement stimulated by thought, seeing it all as like bubbles, flecks of foam, or flowers in the sky. Even when you are not deliberately practicing self-examination, on the surface it seems like all of this is a linear continuity of activity; in reality what we call our activity is just like an electric current, like a wheel of fire, like flowing water: it only constitutes a single linear continuity by virtue of the connecting of countless successive thoughts. Ultimately there is no real thing at all therein. Therefore you will naturally come to feel that mountains are not mountains, rivers are not rivers, the body is not the body, the mind is not the mind. Every bit of all of this is just a dreamlike floating and sinking in the world, that is all. Thus you will spontaneously understand "enlivening the mind without dwelling on anything." In reality, this is already the subtle function of "arousing the mind fundamentally having no place of abode."

Step Five

Next, after you can maintain this state where you have clarified the consciousness and thinking in your mind, you should preserve this radiant, numinous awareness all the time, whether in the midst of stillness or in the midst of activity, maintaining it like a clear sky extending thousands of miles, not keeping any obscuring phenomena in your mind. Then when you have fully experienced this, you will finally be able to understand the truth of human life, and find a state of peace that is a true refuge. But you should not take this condition to be the clarification of mind and perception of essential nature to which Zen refers! And you should not take this to be the enlightenment to which Zen refers! The reason for this is because at this time there exists the function of radiant awareness, and you still don't know its comings and goings, and where it arises. This time is precisely what Han-shan, the great Ming dynasty master, meant when he said, "It is easy to set foot in a forest of thorns; it is hard to turn around at the window screen shining in the moonlight."

In all of what I have said here, I have provisionally used a relatively modern method of explaining the conditions of human psychological activities and states. At the same time I have used this to explain what transpired when the sixth patriarch of Zen experienced an awakening on hearing someone recite the line of the *Diamond sutra* which says, "Enliven the mind without dwelling on anything." If through this you can understand the process of inner work and mental realization represented by the verse composed by the sixth patriarch's senior colleague Shen-hsiu, "The body is the tree of enlightenment, the mind is like a bright mirror stand; wipe it off diligently time and again, not letting it gather dust," then you can thereby know the sixth patriarch's realm of mental realization as represented by his verse, "Enlightenment basically has no tree, and the bright mirror has no stand; originally there is not a single thing, so where can dust gather?" If you make a comparison between these two, you will naturally be able to understand why the fifth patriarch Hung-jen summoned the sixth patriarch to his room in the third watch of the night and entrusted him with the robe and bowl.

However, "Originally there is not a single thing, so where can dust gather," still represents his attainment before he received the transmission of the robe and bowl. Don't forget the states mentioned above, because the state of "originally there is not a single thing" is like the realm of apricot blossoms in the snowy moonlight, which although clear and refined, is after all only one side of the matter, the silent cold of empty silence devoid of any living potential. The time the sixth patriarch made a complete breakthrough to great enlightenment was when he went into the fifth patriarch's room in the third watch of the night, and the fifth patriarch questioned him closely about "enlivening the mind without dwelling on anything," forcing him to go a step further to understand thoroughly the ultimate basis of the essential nature of mind. That is why he said, "Who would have expected that intrinsic nature is fundamentally pure of itself? Who would have expected that intrinsic nature is fundamentally unborn and unperishing? Who would have expected that intrinsic nature is fundamentally complete in itself? Who would have expected that intrinsic nature is fundamentally immovable? Who would have expected that intrinsic nature can produce myriad phenomena?" This finally represents the realm of immediacy and enlightenment in the "sudden enlightenment at a word" spoken of in Zen.

But it will not do to forget how the sixth patriarch lived in hiding among a group of hunters after that, spending fifteen years at sustained cultivation after his enlightenment. By this it can be understood how the

Lankavatara sutra brings up both the sudden and the gradual, and Zen includes both the sudden and the gradual. As it is said in the *Surangama sutra,* "The principle is to be understood all at once; then, using this understanding to clear them up, phenomena are to be worked on gradually, exhausted through a step-by-step process." This indicates the equal importance of sudden and gradual. Nowadays people who talk about Zen studies cling to this one phrase "originally there is not a single thing," and are liable to do just about anything; it's a wonder they don't fall into the views of crazy Zen! You must know that Zen actually has a rigorous process of practical work, and is not a matter of empty talk or wild self-approval; only then can you approach authentic Zen.

The Second Issue

The second issue has to do with the expression "don't think of good, don't think of evil." In the story of the sixth patriarch's enlightenment, I spoke of what transpired when the monk Hui-ming caught up with the sixth patriarch on the Ta-yu Range and declared he had come for the Way rather than to take the robe and bowl. The sixth patriarch therefore first told him, "Don't think of good, don't think of evil." After quite a long while, the sixth patriarch then asked him, "At precisely this moment, what is your original face?" In other words, he was asking, "When you are not thinking of good or evil in your heart, and there is no thinking going on in your mind at all, what is your original face?"

Because very few of the later readers of the *Altar Sutra of the Sixth Patriarch* have done any real Zen work, they overlook the meaning of the expression "quite a long while." And they also take the interrogative "what" in "what is your original face" and read it as if it were the demonstrative "that." Thus they suppose that when this mind is "not thinking of good and not thinking of evil," this itself is the fundamental basis of the essential nature of mind. Hence there has come to be the misunderstanding that recognition of the absence of good and evil is itself the essence of mind. If this be so, can mentally retarded people, mentally ill people who have lost the power of coherent thinking, and brain damaged people all be considered to have attained the realm of Zen?

Thus it should be clear to you that when you reach the point at which you are "not thinking of good and not thinking of evil," only when the open clarity of your mental state produces the realm of all subtle understanding can it be considered the initial enlightenment of Zen. And this can only be said to be initial enlightenment; this is the beginning of what the sixth patriarch referred to as the secret being in you. If people misunderstand this story, they are really in danger of fooling themselves and misleading others; that is why I have made a particular point of presenting this to you for you to reflect upon.

The Third Issue

The third issue has to do with "it is not the wind moving, nor is it the pennant moving; it is your minds moving." This is the sixth patriarch's first exercise of his potential after having just emerged from the mountains, and it is an example of what was called acuity of mind in later Zen. It is a kind of subtle saying characteristic of the situational teaching method; it is not the essential teaching of Zen that points to clarification of mind and perception of its nature. It is equivalent to the saying that "wine does not intoxicate people, people intoxicate themselves; sex does not delude people, people delude themselves," which are similar witticisms.

"When the clouds race by, the moon runs swiftly; when the shoreline shifts, the boat is traveling." Can you tell who is moving and who is still? If you are asleep, even if "on both banks the cries of the monkeys go on and on; the light boat has already passed the myriad mountains," nevertheless you do not see or hear; so how could you compose such a marvelous expression? This is what is referred to in the Only Consciousness doctrine of Buddhism as the wind of objects blowing the waves of consciousness, the principle that all feelings and thoughts are dependent on something else, stirred up by the wind of external objects. It is not the essence of mind of Zen Buddhism, the completely real nature of mind that has the same root as the universe and all things.

Some people often take up the saying "it is your minds moving," from the story of the wind and the pennant, and equate it with having attained complete understanding of the mind teaching of Zen. That is really a hundred and eighty thousand miles from Zen. If it were so, would modern psychological analysis not be sufficient to reach the realm of Zen? What further need would there be to talk about Zen? If you look at the great Zen masters of the T'ang and Sung dynasties in terms of this manner of understanding, you would certainly have to scorn Zen as a useless practice. Just like "a row of white herons rising into the blue sky," the farther the flight, the more remote it becomes!

CHAPTER 9

*The Great Flourishing of Zen
in the Early T'ang Dynasty*

The time of the first widespread preaching of Zen by Hui-neng, the sixth patriarch of the Zen school, corresponds to the reigns of the T'ang dynasty Emperor Kao-tsung (649–683) and Empress Wu Tse-t'ien (684–701). Now if we want to talk about the history of the flourishing of Zen, we must proceed from a simple understanding of the trends in T'ang dynasty Chinese Buddhism as well as T'ang dynasty culture in general.

In the period prior to this time, Chinese culture remained stagnant in an enervated and decadent state, because the people of the Six dynasties were fond of effete literature, elegant but insubstantial, thus creating superficial and unrealistic scholarship and thought. From the early T'ang dynasty, however, through the efforts of the first two T'ang emperors to promote a reform of the Six dynasties literary style, there came to be new life in literature as a tool of expressing ideas.

As to Chinese Buddhism, after the Great Master Chih-che founded the T'ien-t'ai school around the turn of the Ch'en and Sui dynasties, using a scholastic method of critical comparison and orderly arrangement to establish a complete system of Buddhism, a while later Dharma Master Hsuan-tsang returned to China after twenty years of study in India. Given a grand welcome by the government and the people, Hsuan-tsang infused new blood into Chinese Buddhism. Emperor T'ai-tsung of T'ang (r. 626–649) ordered the court to set up a place for Hsuan-tsang to work on translations, thus establishing a translation bureau. There he assembled more than a thousand native scholars and distinguished monks, including monks from Central Asia learned in Sanskrit, as well as priests from the West who had come to China in the early T'ang dynasty to spread the Manichaean doctrines. All of them collaborated in the work of translating Buddhist scriptures.

To translate the Buddhist scriptures, first the individuals in charge of the Sanskrit text and the chief editors of the Chinese version would translate a passage; then in front of the committee they would read out the original meaning of the Sanskrit together with the Chinese translation. Whenever they ran into a passage that was questionable, they would weigh each word and measure each phrase; only after going through a long process of discussion and debate would they make a final decision. This is not like the way we translate Western literature today, with everything coming from the views and understanding of single individuals, so that all sorts of mistakes and oversights occur, resulting in the criticism that translators are drawing tigers that look like dogs.

Through the development of this translation work by Dharma Master Hsuan-tsang, in which he rendered the literature of Only Consciousness, characteristics of phenomena, and logic, the intellectual theory of Buddhist studies established a strict logical system. At the same time, this influenced scholarship in general, which naturally placed emphasis on precisely detailed analysis along with plain and simple expression.

The evolution of fashions and cultural trends in a society of any given age are never formed by just one or two causes. Anything that occurs in the same era is capable of producing, to a greater or lesser extent, an effect that influences the times. If we were to set aside Dharma Master Hsuan-tsang's religious standpoint and look at his work only from the point of view of cultural development, we would have to say that his contribution to T'ang dynasty culture and scholarship was as fine as that of Wei Ch'eng or Fang Hsuan-ling, but the remaining effect of his work has lasted longer than that of either of those two.

Thus it is possible to understand the transmission of Shakyamuni Buddha's doctrines and ideas into China from the end of the Eastern Han dynasty through the Wei, Chin, and Northern and Southern dynasties, up to the early T'ang period. Going through several hundred years of interaction and commingling, like mixing water and milk, eventually it developed entirely into Chinese Buddhism. Dharma Master Hsuan-tsang's work translating Buddhist scriptures can be said to be the definitive conclusion of the transformation of Indian Buddhism into Chinese Buddhism. The life of wisdom in Buddhist studies after that depended completely on dissemination and enhancement by Chinese monks and scholars.

In those times, there were sects of Chinese Buddhism that focused on teaching methods for the practical cultivation of actual realization. First there was the Pure Land school founded by Dharma Master Hui-yuan in the Chin dynasty, which became popular among all classes of people throughout the country. Later, the T'ien-t'ai school founded by Great Master Chih-che of the Sui dynasty took root in the minds of people with respect to the theory and practical methods of realization. Then there entered the doctrines of Only Consciousness and characteristics of phenomena transmitted by Dharma Master Hsuan-tsang, which enshrouded the general run of intellectuals and literati, as well as distinguished Buddhist monks and scholars, in an atmosphere of research and reflection on the subtle principles of Buddhism.

As I have said before, the final goal of Buddhism places importance on the practical and the experiential; it is not ultimately just a matter of professing doctrine or philosophy. By the early T'ang dynasty, the great Buddhists had gone as far as they could in lecturing on doctrines and writing vast tomes. However, they had a strong inclination to turn it all into philosophical thinking and logical deliberation to such a degree that it tended to lose connection with the aim of practical cultivation of true realization.

Then Great Master Bodhidharma transmitted the Zen teaching of practice and realization in the time of Emperor Wu; it was handed on, generation to generation, until by the time of the early T'ang dynasty nearly a century later, the Zen teaching of direct pointing to the human mind to see its essence and attain Buddhahood had gradually become known to people all over. Thus it was that when it reached the time of the sixth patriarch Hui-neng and his colleague Shen-hsiu, the simplified quintessential Zen Way naturally became popular in response to the trends of the times. It was easily accepted by the people, who now took to it with alacrity; so in one leap it became the heart of Chinese Buddhism.

When it comes to the history of the development of the Zen school, most people place overwhelming emphasis on the lineage of Zen transmitted by the sixth patriarch at Ts'ao-ch'i, and do not understand the whole picture. In reality, the Zen that influenced central and northern China from the early T'ang dynasty to the time of its full flourishing was mostly empowered by teachers and disciples who were descended from the fourth and fifth patriarchs, including the sixth patriarch's elder colleague Shen-hsiu.

It was not until the late T'ang, the Five dynasties, and the Northern and Southern Sung dynasties that the five sects of Zen descended from the lineage of the sixth patriarch came to exert the dominant influence in Buddhism and Zen. Among them, the ones whose achievements set up the bridge and built the beacon of the Hui-neng's Southern school of sudden enlightenment were Ma-tsu Tao-i, a successor in the second generation after the sixth patriarch, and Ma-tsu's disciple Pai-chang Huai-hai, who established the Chan (Zen) commune system. If, as has happened, people attribute the flourishing of the Zen school in the lineage of the sixth patriarch to his youngest disciple Shen-hui alone, that is so biased and careless as to be unworthy of serious consideration.

During the early T'ang dynasty, Zen won the esteem of all levels of society due to cooperating factors during the time, as well as the preaching of the disciples of the fifth patriarch who were contemporaries of the sixth patriarch. This enabled the reputation and educational influence of Zen to extend and develop the power of its dissemination everywhere. From the times of the T'ang Emperor Kao-tsung and Empress Wu Tse-t'ien, aside from the sixth patriarch's senior colleague Shen-hsiu, who had already been made a "National Teacher" of the court, a number of Zen masters were made National Teachers such as Hui-an of Sung-yueh and Wei-cheng, who were heirs of a branch succession from the fifth patriarch, and Tao-chin, who was an heir of a branch succession from the fourth patriarch. The simultaneous arising of the Hua-yen school was also very much connected with the Zen masters of the lineage of the fourth and fifth patriarchs.

As for the Zen way of the sixth patriarch Hui-neng, it started spreading from Ling-nan from the time of Empress Wu Tse-t'ien to the reign of Emperor Hsuan-tsung (713–755), gradually reaching throughout the areas of Hunan and Kiangsi, south of the Yangtse River. The disciples of the school of the sixth patriarch mostly stayed in the mountains and forests, concentrating on cultivating Zen tranquility. Very few of them were like the masters of northern and central China who became famous and exerted a great effect on the intelligentsia and commoners alike.

But since the sixth patriarch set the example of not making use of lofty or profound doctrines, just employing everyday speech to express the mental essence of Buddhism, the style of the sudden teaching of the Southern school of Zen was henceforth established by his later heirs such as Ma-tsu Tao-i and Pai-chang Huai-hai. Whether engaged in dialogue or in explaining the Dharma, they commonly used colloquial speech and local expressions. Their subtle words were ungraspable but as valuable as pearls. Only by inner understanding integrated into ordinary life was it possible to understand the essence of their way. They took the profound doctrines of the majestic, solemn, and sacred Buddhist scriptures and turned them into a light and witty manner of teaching that made its revelations according to the situation. This was the beginning of Zen studies in Chinese culture, and it was also a revolutionary change toward ordinariness in Buddhism. This produced a number of particular points of dissimilarity between Zen and Buddhism, which I will reintroduce later.

Coming to the late T'ang, the Five dynasties, and the Northern and Southern Sung dynasties, besides the aforementioned conditions, Zen also had an inseparable connection with vernacular literature. The spiritual talks of the Zen masters produced many flavorful and idiomatic rhymes and verses that influenced the peculiar forms and meters of poetry in Sung dynasty literature. Although the literature of the Ming and Ch'ing dynasties inherited this influence, it already had a feeling of imitation, which is an obvious mark of inferiority.

When we have a clear picture of the arising of Zen from the early T'ang dynasty onward, and the pattern of its change, we can understand that the controversy between the sudden Zen of the south and the gradual Zen of the north is not an important issue in Zen history. It will not do to miss the great on account of the small, just going up blind alleys searching out fragmentary and biased source materials to come up with apparently new and different views.

For example, the business of the sixth patriarch's minor disciple Shen-hui (Ho-tse) going to the capital to fight for the political status of the Zen school had no effect or influence on the authentic Zen masters who were truly devoted to seeking the Way, and left society without anxiety to conceal their tracks in the mountains and forests. Indeed, according to what is recorded in Zen historical sources, Shen-hui went to the capital at that time because the gradualistic school of Sung-yueh was popular; this aroused his indignation and motivated him to write *Notice Revealing the Source.*

Shen-hui went through considerable effort before he finally established the idea of two schools of Zen in the year 745: the Southern school of sudden enlightenment associated with Hui-neng, and the Northern school of gradual cultivation associated with Shen-hsiu. In reality, the Zen of Sung-yueh had emerged from transmissions of branch lineages descended from the fourth and fifth patriarchs of Zen, which had little relation to Shen-hsiu.

Furthermore, gradual cultivation and sudden enlightenment are originally like the two wheels of the one cart of Zen. Shen-hui did something uncalled for, and got nothing more than a vain reputation much like that of any worldling. What has that to do with authentic Zen and Zen masters? This is why the great Zen masters in the south at that time never said a word about this. So we know it is a problem where there is no problem, and indeed a small issue where there is no issue. How is it even worth talking about?

Zen after the sixth patriarch made progress through the spontaneous promotion and esteem of the people, and was not based on establishments made by the powers of emperors, kings, and governments. Because it involves "learning from below to arrive up above," it later became universally recognized by all classes throughout the country as the most excellent and most special school of Buddhism. To put it in a proverb after the manner of a phrase of Buddhist scripture, "It was most extraordinarily special and unusual."

PART IV
Some Keys to Studying Zen

CHAPTER 10

On the Use of Colloquialisms

After the sixth patriarch, Zen spread widely in southern China from the time of the flourishing of the T'ang dynasty, gradually transforming the method of teaching that had carried on for hundreds of years since Buddhism came to the country. It took the subtle doctrines of the five or six thousand volumes of Buddhist classics—the scriptures, rules of behavior, treatises, and the twelve sections of these three treasuries of the canon—and reduced them to a specially transmitted teaching outside of doctrine, represented by the Buddha twirling a flower and Kasyapa smiling. Thus it is that Zen makes a special presentation of the central issue of "directly pointing to the human mind for perception of its essence and attainment of Buddhahood."

An additional factor in this transformation was the fact that the sixth patriarch was unschooled and illiterate, so whenever he was communicating the Zen mind essence he did not use the format of interpreting doctrines according to writings, glossing characters, and annotating scriptures. He just used ordinary expressions to point at the reality of mind with direct precision, which happened to accord with the principle of seeking realization through direct transmission and reception of clarifying mind, and seeing its essence, as illustrated by the saying that Zen was "specially transmitted outside of doctrine, not setting up words."

Then when it came into the hands of the disciples in the second generation after the sixth patriarch, they spontaneously formulated a kind of mode or style characteristic of the school of Sudden Enlightenment in the Southern tradition of Hui-neng. Although the source materials of Zen left to us today do contain infinite value, nevertheless when you read Zen books you have the feeling that they are so vague you don't know what they are saying. Because I want young people today engaged in the same study to know the treasures of Chinese culture, I must explain certain points that have to be recognized at the outset.

Zen books are usually collections on individual Zen masters, so they are called "records of sayings." These records of sayings are everyday talks on Zen study, with questions and answers on doubts and problems. They are comparatively straightforward and free from rhetorical embellishment, recording the Zen masters' day-to-day talks and lectures. Like the Altar Sutra of the Sixth Patriarch, for example, they do their best to avoid profound Buddhist doctrines and literary conceits. Because of this, the records of sayings are largely in the vernacular languages of the T'ang and Sung dynasties. To study them, it is therefore essential to be especially aware of the use of T'ang dynasty colloquialisms and terms from the dialects of such regions as Hunan, Hupei, Kiangsi, Fukien, and Canton, as well as the old pronunciation resembling that of the Chinese heartland during the T'ang dynasty.

At the same time it is essential to understand that the appearance of the Zen school records of sayings was also a revolution in the attitude of Chinese culture toward scholastic method. The records of sayings, the literary style of the Sung dynasty neo-Confucians, were derived from this very source. In reality, the formation of the conversational style of the records of sayings also had two remote causes. For one thing, it was itself a derivation from Buddhist scriptures, which are originally question-and-answer dialogues. Second, it was also derived from an evolution of Chinese culture. In traditional Chinese culture, the *Analects* of Confucius and the *New Words on Worldly Talks* by Liu I-ch'ing (fl. ca. 420) of the Liu Sung dynasty were both very important. The conversational style of the records of sayings was born of a combination of the spirit of these two works.

From the Sung dynasty on, the Zen schools had edited records of sayings and compiled them in massive collections such as the *Records of Transmission of the Lamp, Eye of Humanity and Heaven, Five Lamps Merged in the Source, Records of Pointing at the Moon,* and other works including the imperial selection compiled in the Ying-cheng era (1723–1735) by the emperor of the Ch'ing dynasty. All of these Zen classics are anthologies containing principles, literary illustrations, studies of sources, and many other valuable materials for Zen study. If you want to study Zen, *Records of Transmission of the Lamp, Records of Pointing at the Moon,* and *Imperial Selection of Sayings* are all essential reading. To make a thorough and detailed study, it is necessary to read through the individual sayings of all the Zen masters.

CHAPTER 11

Understanding Some Important Technical Terms

Public Cases

In the Zen records of sayings, stories from the history of the school are called *kung-an*, or public cases. The use of the term "study cases" by the Sung dynasty neo-Confucians was also derived from this. Zen masters from the Sung dynasty on had an expression "raising the ancient," which referred to the practice of taking up a story of the quest, enlightenment, or teaching method of one of the ancient Zen masters, and using it as material for explanation, discussion, investigation, or for stimulating doubt. This has a meaning similar to the expression "discussing the ancient" used in modern Chinese agricultural society. There is also an expression "versifying the ancient," which means taking up the essential point of an old public case and composing a critical or laudatory verse on it in order to resolve the doubts of students, as seen in the following examples.

Here is a verse on a public case of the sixth patriarch, composed by Zen Master Huang-lung Ssu-hsin Wu-hsin:

> *The sixth patriarch was not a great man back then*
> *When he had somebody write that gibberish on*
>   *the wall.*
> *Clearly he had a verse saying there is no thing;*
> *Yet he received the other's single bowl.*

Here is a comment by Zen Master Ta-hui Tsung-kao on Huang-lung's verse regarding the case of the sixth patriarch:

> *Tell me, is the bowl a thing or not? If you say it is a*
> *thing, then old Ssu-hsin is not a great man either. If*
> *you say it is not a thing, what can you do about the*
> *bowl?*

Here is a verse by Master Hsiu-shan on the sixth patriarch's case of the wind and the pennant:

> *When the wind blows, the mind moves the trees;*
> *When clouds arise, essence rouses dust.*
> *If you understand today's affair,*
> *You obscure the original human being.*

The Sharp Point of Potential

The sharp point of potential in Zen is a favorite topic among those who talk about and lecture on Zen studies. In reality, the cause of hindrance to the life of wisdom in Zen, and the reason why study of Zen can easily get into vain sidetracks, is precisely the error of later people in being too fond of the sharp point of potential.

119

The sixth patriarch was originally the first to show hints of the sharp point of potential; then it was transformed in the hands of the Masters Ma-tsu Tao-i, Pai-chang, Huang-po, and Lin-chi, becoming intensified and forming the newest and most outstanding teaching method in the T'ang and Sung dynasties. Buddhism originally had a technical term known as "corresponding to potential," which referred to a basic principle of teaching method.

The word "potential" in Buddhism has several meanings in the context of teaching method, including the student's natural endowments and power of learning, as well as the spontaneous opportunities that arise in daily life which can be employed to help a student awaken. The expression "corresponding to potential" refers to a basic principle of teaching method that must be taken seriously by anyone who is working as a teacher.

In the hands of the Zen masters, who brought forth the living application of Zen whenever they lectured and taught, the methods and sayings they used to open up the insight of students were all like marvelous pearls rolling in a dish, a sight totally unique and unlike anything else in the world. These were the sharp points of potential. This simile also sums up the quintessential meaning of both the sharp points of potential and pivotal sayings used by Zen masters since the T'ang and Sung dynasties, including the operation of the Zen teaching method wherein there is a sense of swiftness and sharpness, like the tip of an arrow, and a sense of the Taoist butcher cutting up oxen without holding the concept of a full grown ox in his mind. And this also happens to be like the function of the teaching method spoken of by Confucius in these terms: "If not aroused, they do not awaken; if not dumbstruck, they do not open up."

If we view the context of question-and-answer dialogues in terms of the operation of points of potential, sometimes it is explaining something wrong in such a way as to make it right, or explaining something right in such a way as to show how it is wrong. Sometimes it is expressing agreement, sometimes it is expressing denial. It never follows any fixed rule, but whatever it may be, the purpose is to test students' perception and realization, and to arouse their doubts in such a way as to induce them to seek on their own, awaken on their own, and reach agreement on their own.

Because of this, the sharp points of potential and the pivotal sayings of the Zen masters often may be thoroughly unexpected and unthinkable by ordinary convention, even cryptic or humorous, with an endless potential of application to various situations. But they are all situational responses and never prefabrications; every word flows from natural reality. Their operation is all in the representation of the speech, silence, or action of a given time and place; it does not mean that people studying Zen must always and everywhere be engrossed in points of potential and subtle sayings.

From the Ming and Ch'ing dynasties onward, Zen degenerated. Often there were religious transmissions by phony Zen masters who would first make up a verse-like canto, expressing sharpness of wit, to use as a fetish in religious transmission. Some would even request a specialist to compose such cantos for them to recite which they had put down as records of their own sayings to be transmitted to later generations. That such fondness for fame should even reach beyond conventional society is extremely lamentable.

But nowadays people who study Zen all take the subtle usages of sharp points of potential and pivotal sayings to be the heart of Zen. They talk about the stories and sharp wits of the ancient Zen masters and even claim that the essence of Zen is represented entirely therein. Is this not a matter for regret? The Sung dynasty Zen Master Hsueh-tou Ch'ung-hsien had already composed some verses criticizing students who became attached to Zen in this way:

> *A rabbit lies across an ancient road;*
> *A hawk sees it at a glance and captures it alive.*
> *What a pity the hunting dog is not too keen;*
> *All it does is sniff around a withered tree stump.*
>
> *Decrepit old Yun-men sails an iron boat;*
> *South of the river and north of the river, they struggle*
>   *to see.*
> *What a pity so many people casting their hooks*
> *Stand there in rows absentminded, losing their*
>   *fishing rods.*
>
> *Spinning like jades and pearls, the words of*
>   *Buddhas and Masters;*
> *Even to understand thoroughly defiles the field of mind.*
> *Old Lu only knows how to keep on polishing rice;*
> *How could that fashion be transmitted through*
>   *the ages?*

(In the poem, Yun-men was a Sung dynasty master, Yun-men Wen-yen. "Old Lu" refers to the sixth patriarch of Zen, whose lay surname was Lu.)

Example One: An Ordinary Sharp Point of Potential

When Zen Master Fa-ch'ang of Mount Ta-mei first called on Ma-tsu, he asked, "What is Buddha?" Ma-tsu replied, "Mind is Buddha," whereupon the master was greatly enlightened. During the Teng-yuan era of the T'ang dynasty (785–804) he lived on Mount Ta-mei (Giant Apricot Mountain). During that time a monk from the community of Zen Master Yen-kuan, who had gone into the mountains to cut a staff, lost his way and came upon Master Fa-ch'ang's hut.

The monk asked the master, "How long have you been living on this mountain?"

The master replied, "I only see the surrounding mountains become green and then yellow."

The monk then asked, "Which way is the path out of the mountains?"

The master answered, "Along with the flow."

When the monk got back, he told Yen-kuan about this. Yen-kuan mused, "When I was in Kiangsi I once saw a certain monk, but I have never heard what became of him since. I wonder if that's who it is." The upshot of it was that he had the monk go invite the master to come out of the mountains, but the master composed a verse saying,

> *A broken down withered tree stays in a cold forest;*
> *How many times has it met the spring without a*
> *   change of heart?*
> *Even the woodcutters that come across it pay no*
> *   attention;*
> *Why should a plasterer bother to search it out?*

When Ma-tsu heard that the master was living on the mountain, he also sent a monk there to ask, "What did you attain when you saw Ma-tsu, that you came to live on this mountain?"

The master replied, "Ma-tsu told me that mind is Buddha, and so I live here."

The monk then said, "Ma-tsu's Buddhism is different these days."

The master asked, "How is it different?"

The monk answered, "Recently he has also been saying 'neither mind nor Buddha.'"

The master responded, "That old fellow never ceases to confuse people. You can have your 'neither mind nor Buddha.' I am only interested in mind being Buddha."

When that monk went back and told Ma-tsu about this, Ma-tsu said, "Everyone, the 'Apricot' is ripe!"

Example Two: Sharp Points of Potential Giving Wordless Teaching, Breaking Down an Inadequate View on the Part of a Student, and Showing How the Manner of Teaching of Two Great Masters Accords Without Contrivance

When Teng-feng was leaving Ma-tsu, Ma-tsu asked him, "Where are you going?"

Teng-feng said, "To Shih-t'ou." (Shih-t'ou was another name of Zen Master Hsi-ch'ien, a colleague of Ma-tsu.)

Ma-tsu warned, "The road of Shih-t'ou is slippery."

Replied Teng-feng, "My acrobatic pole is always with me; I perform wherever I am." Then he left.

As soon as Teng-feng reached Shih-t'ou, he walked around the meditation seat once, shook his staff once, and asked, "What doctrine is this?" Shih-t'ou cried,

"Heavens! Heavens!" As a result, Teng-feng was speechless. He returned to Ma-tsu and told him about this.

Ma-tsu advised, "You should go question him again, and when he answers, you should whistle twice." So Teng-feng went again to question Shih-t'ou as before, but Shih-t'ou answered him by whistling twice. Again Teng-feng was speechless. When he went back and told master Ma-tsu, Ma-tsu only said, "I told you the road of Shih-t'ou is slippery!"

Example Three: Sharp Points of Potential Guiding in Accordance with the Situation

Li Ao first saw Zen Master Yao-shan when Li was serving a term as inspector of Lang province. Li noticed the Zen master's teaching and invited the master to call on him many times. But the master never responded, so he went to call on the master himself.

When Li Ao arrived, Yao-shan was holding a scroll of scripture and paid no attention to the government official. The Zen master's attendant then announced, "The governor is here." But Li had an impatient temperament and because he had been ignored, he snapped, "Seeing the face is not as good as hearing the name," and left abruptly.

The Zen master then said, "How can the governor value his ears but demean his eyes?" Hearing this, Li came back and apologized, and then asked, "What is the Way?" Pointing up and down, the master said, "Do you understand?" "No," replied Li. The master responded, "The clouds are in the blue sky, the water's in the pitcher." Li thereupon joyfully bowed to the master, and presented a verse of praise:

He's refined his physical form into one like that of a crane;
Under a stand of a thousand pines, two boxes of scripture.
I come and ask about the Way, he says nothing extra:
"The clouds are in the blue sky, the water's in the pitcher."

Li also asked, "What are discipline, concentration, and insight?" Master Yao-shan answered, "This poor wayfarer has no such excess furniture here." Li could not fathom the inner message of this answer at which the Zen master told him, "Governor, if you wish to preserve this thing, you must stand on the summit of the highest mountain and walk on the bottom of the deepest sea. You cannot even let go of things at home, so your mental energy leaks and drains."

Li later presented another poem, which said,

He's chosen a recondite abode, to suit his rustic feelings;
Throughout the year he sees none off and welcomes none.
Sometimes he ascends directly to the summit of the lone
*   peak;*
Cutting through the clouds under the moon, the solitary
*   sound of his whistle.*

After the Sung dynasty minister Chang Shang-ying had attained awakening through Zen study, he composed a verse on the story of Li Ao seeing Yao-shan.

The clouds are in the blue sky, the water is in the pitcher.
If the light of the eyes follows the point finger, it
*   falls in a deep pit.*
The valley flowers cannot withstand the pain of
*   wind and frost;*
How can you talk about walking the floor of the
*   deepest sea?*

These three examples elucidate the mode of sharp points of potential used by the Zen masters. There are also many others, too numerous to mention. To sum up, sharp points of potential were an expedient device used by Zen masters to expound reality, a kind of teaching method using situational education. But they are not the message or purpose of Zen at all. They are only a practical methodology that changes according to the time, place, and people, and are not ultimate principles. If people who study Zen concentrate solely on sharp points of potential and pivotal sayings, that is like the Chinese joke about mistakenly taking chicken feathers for the arrow of leadership.

Caning and Shouting

People often associate Zen with caning and shouting, as though caning and shouting were inseparable from Zen. In reality, caning and shouting are just one type of applied teaching method used by the Zen masters as containing the meaning of the educational spirit of the *Book of Rites*.

In ancient China, hitting was sometimes used in teaching lessons, and this developed into admonitory caning. After Chinese Buddhism had its days of greatest glory through the Zen school, having gone through the structural changes instituted by Ma-tsu and Pai-chang who had founded the communal system where people lived together to cultivate Zen practice, the great Zen masters who had real insight and really applied it in practice would often attract followings of hundreds or even a thousand people of different kinds. As it is said, "Dragons and snakes were mixed up, ordinary people and sages lived together."

Therefore, it was inevitable that things would become mixed up when there were so many people staying together. Because of this, several of the great masters of the T'ang and Sung dynasties liked to keep a Zen staff in their hands, using it as a symbol of leadership, with its authority and good faith. When it was necessary, the staff could also be used as an admonishing cane, in the manner of the ruler carried by schoolteachers forty or fifty years ago. But in reality, a Zen master's cane was not used to hit people all the time; only during periods of problem study was it sometimes used to make a light gesture symbolizing reward or punishment. In the schools of later eras, when people studying Zen with a master would get nailed or put down, this was called "taking a beating." Now when we modern-day folks use the expression "getting nailed," does that mean that there is really a nail that gets hammered in?

As for the famous Zen "shout," this is an exclamation used like the cane to represent a sense of reward or punishment. The "caning and shouting" of Zen came from the fondness of Zen Master Te-shan for using the cane, and the fondness of Zen Master Lin-chi for using the shout. Therefore, in later Zen we find the traditional classic expressions of "the cane of Te-shan, the shout of Lin-chi, the cake of Yun-men, and the tea of Chao-chou."

In sum, caning and shouting were practical applications of a teaching method, in which a light stroke of the cane could represent reward, punishment, or neither reward nor punishment. In later schools they had the terms, but not the reality. Among the older masters I have seen, sometimes when they recognized an error in a student's knowledge or vision, they just laughed at the student without giving any approval or disapproval. Some would just sit there with their eyes closed, remaining silent and giving no answer. These are the relics of caning and shouting. In the past when I ran into this sort of situation, I looked into myself once again, and if I found I was wrong, I let them strike the blow.

This is a most difficult educational method to apply in actual practice. Unless one is a genuine master with highly developed talents and great virtues, there is really no way to carry it out. Therefore, at the height of the great T'ang dynasty, Zen Master Huang-po said, "There are no Zen teachers in all of T'ang China!" Someone asked him how he could say this in view of the fact that there were currently Zen teachers everywhere one went. Huang-po simply replied, "I don't say there is no Zen, just that there are no teachers."

Because of this, Huang-po's approved disciple, Master Lin-chi I-hsuan, who was later to become the founding patriarch of the Lin-chi school of Zen, explained the capacities and conditions necessary for being a Zen master: as he said, "Sometimes I first observe and then act, sometimes I first act and then observe. Sometimes observation and action are simultaneous, sometimes observation and action are not simultaneous. When observation precedes action, the person is still there. When action precedes observation, the phenomenon is still there. When observation and action are simultaneous, they drive off the plowman's ox, take away the hungry man's food, tap the bones and take the marrow, thrusting the needle in sharply. When observation and action are not simultaneous, there are questions and there are answers, it is established who is the guest and it is established who is the host; mixing in the water and joining in the mud, they are used to deal with people according to potential. If one is beyond measure, one will get up and act on it before it is even mentioned. That would be getting somewhere."

Lin-chi also had an explanation for the beating and shouting: "Sometimes I take away the subject but not the object; sometimes I take away the object but not the subject. Sometimes both subject and object are taken away together, and sometimes neither subject nor object are taken away."

Someone asked about taking away the subject but not the object. Lin-chi said, "The warm sun arouses the birth of brocade spread upon the earth; the baby's hair hanging down is white as silk thread."

Someone asked about taking away the object but not the subject. Lin-chi said, "The royal command has already been executed throughout the land; the general outside the borders is freed from the smoke and dust."

Someone asked about taking away both subject and object at once. Lin-chi said, "The whole region has cut off communications and occupies one realm independently."

Someone asked about taking away neither subject nor object. Lin-chi said, "The king goes up into the jeweled throne room; the old peasants sing joyful songs."

Lin-chi also once said, "Sometimes a shout is like a diamond sword. Sometimes a shout is like a crouching lion. Sometimes a shout is like a sounding device. Sometimes a shout is not used as a shout."

CHAPTER 12

Important Points in Reading Zen Classics

The public cases and sharp points of potential, as well as caning and shouting, belong to the domain of Zen teaching methods. It is imperative to know them, and it is furthermore essential to understand thoroughly where their function lies, as well as the conditions obtaining for the particular time, event, and person for which they were used. Outside of this, however, they are definitely not to be taken for the ultimate message and purpose of Zen as is happening today.

If you really and truly want to understand the essential Zen method of communicating mind, it is particularly necessary to pay attention to the sermons, lectures, informal meetings, evening meetings, and other such summaries of the teaching in the recorded sayings of Zen masters. That is Zen study on comparatively solid ground. But if you want to read these books, you must first have your own foundation of basic Confucian,

131

Buddhist, and Taoist learning. This is especially relevant to Buddhism; you cannot read those books without any knowledge at all, otherwise you'd be like the proverbial "mosquito biting an iron ox," never finding a way to sink in your teeth.

The first example of true Zen study is a sermon given by Zen Master Pai-chang: "The spiritual light shines alone, far beyond senses and objects; the essence reveals true eternity. It is not captured in words. The nature of mind is stainless, fundamentally complete and perfect in itself; just detach from false conditioning, and you merge with the Buddha of suchness as is."

He also said, "All verbal teachings are just remedies to cure illness. Because illnesses are not the same, therefore the remedies are not the same. That is why it is sometimes said that there is Buddha, and sometimes it is said there is no Buddha. True words are those that cure illness; after the illness is cured, all of them are untrue statements. True words are false words insofar as they produce opinions; false words are true words insofar as they stop people's delusions. Because illness is unreal, there are only unreal remedies to cure them."

The second example is an address by Zen Master Tung-shan: "Is there anyone who does not repay the four debts (to the Buddha, to teachers, to the country, and to parents) and the three realms of being (desire, form, and formless)?" No one replied. The master continued, "If you do not understand the meaning of this, how can you transcend the troubles of beginning and end? You must not grasp anything in any state of mind, not be anywhere with every step you take. If you can continue this uninterruptedly, then you will attain accord. You should work hard and not pass the days idly."

In addition to these two sermons, there is a great deal of other material, too much to mention. The individual works of the great Zen masters, including their letters in reply to questions, are all very good sources for Zen study. If you neglect them and do not put them to use, instead just bringing up stories of sharp wit to generalize about Zen, that is running in the opposite direction from the Way. Do not under any circumstances fool people with such stories, for this is really more than a trivial misdeed.

In sum, whether it is in religion or philosophy, education, scholarship, or writing, the real true purpose is to give other people accurate indications of how to live peacefully and meaningfully, how to stand on their own and deal with the world. It is not a matter of deliberately picking things up to give an impression of novelty or uniqueness, saying things people don't understand and then claiming oneself to be high-minded.

The Necessity of Preparatory Learning in Zen and Literature

Zen is of course the peculiarly Chinese form of Chinese Buddhism, but from the point of view of the complete system of Buddhist studies founded by Shakyamuni, its basic message did not fundamentally change Shakyamuni's essential message after it was amalgamated with Chinese culture. What it produced was a form peculiar to Chinese culture in terms of its mode of teaching, its terminology, and its manner of expressing the highest truths, going so far as even absorbing, combining, and borrowing terms and modes from Confucianism and Taoism.

Because of this, when you study Zen, if you do not have a complete understanding of the doctrines of Mahayana and Hinayana Buddhism; read over the canonical Buddhist scriptures, precepts, and treatises; clearly understand the general principles of the schools of Chinese Buddhism; or do not understand the methodology and praxis of concentration and insight cultivated according to Buddhist teachings to seek actual realization, but just speak in terms of the Zen mood, then you will surely be unable to touch upon its central message and the fruit of its path. At the very least you will fall into a state in which you will become more narrow-minded the farther you proceed, and the more you study, the more biased you will become.

Especially now in the present day, when meditation methods similar to Zen concentration, such as those used in Indian yoga, have already spread widely throughout the world, if people talk about Zen without any real experience of practice and realization, it may be contemptuously rejected by those who think it is no more than the babble of occultist charlatans. If you are determined to study Zen, you must embrace the spirit of "being aloof from the world, unknown to others, yet without anxiety," and "being unshakably certain." You certainly should not talk about Zen just because everyone is talking about it; if you will not approach the study with true sincerity, but just aim for "false learning to flatter society," thereby to obtain empty fame for a time, that is an incomparably great loss, both for others and for yourself.

In sum, we should not under any circumstances forget that Zen is based on the teaching of realizing the ineffable heart of nirvana, attaining freedom from birth and death, and transcending things. How could it just be vainly putting forward empty words divorced from the principles of Buddhism?

Next, when we want to make a serious reading of the Zen classics from the T'ang, Sung, and subsequent dynasties, if we do not have the appropriate training in Chinese literature, trying to read those classics will be like, as the ancient Zen masters said, "biting into an iron donut," with no way to sink your teeth in. Zen studies from the mid-T'ang to the Sung, Ming, and Ch'ing dynasties even went a step farther and formed an inseparable relationship with Chinese literature, joining courses with poetry, song, and other forms of literature. Thus, Zen may be extremely hard to understand if you approach its study solely through modern Chinese writings.

Furthermore, in the development of Chinese literature, from the works of the Wei, Chin, and Six dynasties on through the poetry of T'ang, the elegies of Sung, the songs of Yuan, the novels of Ming, and the linking rhymes of Ch'ing, all have a subtle interconnection with states of Zen experience. Therefore, if you want to understand the spirit of Zen studies completely, you must have a certain degree of cultivation in Buddhism and Chinese literature.

Some people still say that the sixth patriarch of Zen, Hui-neng, was originally an illiterate woodcutter, and he didn't need to understand Buddhist doctrine or literature, yet attained enlightenment and became a Buddha and a patriarch just the same. That is true, but how many people were there like Hui-neng before or after the sixth patriarch? Basically, the reality of Buddhahood and Zen enlightenment is in a domain reached by wisdom; intellectual knowledge does not apply here at all, but how many people, after all, are fully endowed with wisdom? If you have a tendency to compare yourself with the sixth patriarch, you are already missing his virtue of modesty, and are already filled with conceit. That is running in the opposite direction from the Way!

Furthermore, when Shakyamuni Buddha expressed the message that is "specially transmitted outside of doctrine and does not set up written formulations," he had already given the countless discourses that formed the content of the sutras. Only after that did he bring forth this mode of sweeping away attachment to words, names, and appearances. It is not that he originally established this doctrine directly and definitively without using words. This point deserves special attention.

In sum, Buddhism and Zen are both methods of teaching that change adaptively according to the time and place. The doings of people with true wisdom are each distinguished in their own way; it is very much better not to try to observe something in progress from a subjectively fixed point of view, for that would result in becoming disoriented every time you turned around. But to learn, and to travel the Way, it is essential to seek what is right in actual fact, proceeding with your feet on the real ground. First seek to enter within, and only then you can go outside. Otherwise you will waste a lifetime of scholarship. That would be most regrettable indeed!

Many stories can be used to illustrate the intimate relationship between Zen and Chinese literature. A first such story concerns Zen Master Te-ch'eng, "the Boatman" of Flower Inn. His discipline and conduct were highly elevated, and he was a man of extraordinary measure. After he had his mind sealed by Zen Master Yao-shan, he became a spiritual associate of Tao-wu and Yun-yen. When it came time for them to leave Master Yao-shan, Te-ch'eng said to his two colleagues, "You two should each stay somewhere to set up the teaching of Yao-shan. I am coarse and rustic by nature, and prefer the mountains and rivers to teaching in the cities; I have no capabilities. Some day when you know that I have a place to stay, if you meet any spiritually sharp professors [in T'ang and Sung dynasty Buddhism they called a priest who lectured on Buddhist scriptures a professor], direct one to me, if he can be polished, and I will pass on what I attained in my life, to return the favor of our own teacher."

Then he parted from his colleagues, and went on alone until he came to Flower Inn. There he lived on a small boat, passing the days according to circumstances and making contact with the people coming and going from the four directions. People of the time, not knowing of his lofty attainments, called him the Boatman monk.

One day, when he had moored his boat and was sitting at leisure on the shore, a certain government official asked him, "What are your daily activities?" The master stood an oar on its end and said, "Understand?" The official responded, "No," so the master replied, "As I negotiate the clear waves, golden fish are rarely encountered."

Later, the Boatman's colleague Tao-wu came to the outskirts of the capital, where he encountered Chia-shan giving a lecture. A monk in the audience asked Chia-shan, "What is the body of reality?" and Chia-shan answered, "The body of reality has no form." The monk asked, "What is the eye of reality?" and Chia-shan replied, "The eye of reality has no flaw." Hearing this, Tao-wu unconsciously let out a laugh.

Chia-shan therefore got down from the platform and inquired of Tao-wu, "There must have been something wrong in my answers to this monk just now, to make you break out into laughter. Please do not spare me your kindness and compassion." Tao-wu said, "You are established in the world; don't you have a teacher?" Chia-shan again entreated Tao-wu, "Where was I wrong? Please tell me." Tao-wu only shook his head, saying, "I'll never tell you. Please go instead to the Boatman at Flower Inn." Chia-shan asked, "What is that man like?" Tao-wu replied, "That man hasn't a single tile over his head, nor a square inch of ground under his feet. If you go there, you should change your attire."

Chia-shan then dismissed the congregation, wrapped himself up in traveling gear, and went right to Flower Inn.

As soon as the Zen Master Boatman saw Chia-shan, he asked him, "Of which temple are you the resident, Great Worthy?"

Chia-shan answered, "Of a temple I am not a resident; dwelling is not becoming."

The Zen master then asked, "Unbecoming in the sense of not being like what?"

Chia-shan replied, "It is a phenomenon before the eyes."

The master said, "Where did you learn it?"

Chia-shan responded, "It is not within reach of ears or eyes."

Then the Zen Master Boatman said, "A single fitting statement is an eternal donkey tethering stake."

Looking at Chia-shan, the Zen Boatman dared, "Trailing the line a thousand fathoms, the intent is in the deep pool; three inches away from the hook, why don't you speak?" As Chia-shan was going to say something, the master hit him with an oar and tumbled him into the water. As soon as Chia-shan hauled himself up into the boat, the master urged him again, "Speak, speak!" Chia-shan tried to say something, but the master hit him again.

Now Chia-shan emptied out and opened up in great enlightenment. He then nodded his head three times. The master then said, "You may play with the line on the fishing rod as you will; without even touching the clear waves, the meaning is distinct of itself."

Chia-shan then asked the master, "What is the master's intention in casting line and hook?"

"The thread hangs down in the green water, the bob determines ideas of being and nothingness," answered Te-ch'eng.

Chia-shan commented, "Speech carries the mystery, yet without a road; the tongue talks, yet without talking."

Hearing this, the master announced, "I have fished all the waves of the river, and this is the first golden fish I've found." Chia-shan covered his ears. The master said, "That's right, that's right," and then gave him this piece of advice: "When you go, you should conceal yourself without any traces, but do not conceal yourself where there are no traces. In the thirty years I was with Yao-shan, I only understood this. Now you have it: hereafter do not live in cities or towns, but only in the deep mountains, with a hoe at your side. Seek someone to continue it, so that it will not die out."

Chia-shan then took his leave and started off, but he kept turning around to look back, so the master called to him, "Reverend!" When Chia-shan turned his head, the master raised the oar and yelled, "Do you think there is something else?" Then he capsized his boat, plunged into the water, and disappeared.

A second example concerns Master Yuan-an of Mount Luo-pu. First he followed Lin-chi, but the circumstances were not met, so he left to go elsewhere. Lin-chi said, "In the school of Lin-chi there is a red-finned carp who wags his head, shakes his tail, and goes off to the south. I don't know whose pickle jar he will wind up in." After Yuan-an had traveled around, he went directly to Mount Chia; there he built a hermitage, but over the years he never went to visit Chia-shan, the Zen master of Mount Chia.

Zen Master Chia-shan consequently prepared a letter, which he had a monk deliver to the hermit. When the hermit received the letter, he immediately sat down and extended his hand again in a gesture of seeking something. The monk had no reply. The hermit tapped him and said, "Go back and tell the master what happened."

The monk went back and recounted this to Chia-shan, who stated, "If the hermit opens the letter, he will come within three days. If he does not open the letter, the man cannot be saved." Then Chia-shan had someone watch the hermitage to see if the hermit would come out, with instructions to burn the hermitage upon his leaving.

Three days later Yuan-an actually left the hermitage. When someone came up to him and told him that his hermitage was on fire, he paid no attention. He went directly to Chia-shan, and, without making any bows, stood right in front of him with his hands in a gesture of greeting. Chia-shan confronted him saying, "A chicken lodging in a phoenix nest is incongruous; get out!"

Yuan-an replied, "I have come from afar pursuing the way; please meet me once."

Chia-shan countered, "There is no you there, and no me here." Then Yuan-an shouted. Chia-shan responded, "Stop, stop! Don't be so crude! They are the same clouds and moon, but the valley and the mountain are different from one another. It is not that you cannot cut off the tongues of everyone on earth, but how can you make a tongueless man speak?" Yuan-an stood there thinking how to answer, whereupon Chia-shan hit him. Because of this Yuan-an became a follower of Chia-shan.

Later he one day asked Chia-shan, "How does one understand the place where neither Buddha nor devil reach?" Chia-shan replied, "A light illumines objects hundreds of miles around; an old monk gets lost in a dark room." Yuan-an also asked, "How is it when the morning sun has risen and the night moon does not appear?" to which Chia-shan said, "The dragon keeps the ocean pearl in its mouth and pays no attention to the sporting fish." At these words, Yuan-an was greatly enlightened.

When Chia-shan was about to die, he uttered these words: "A branch on a stone; look, look—it is dying!"

Yuan-an responded, "Not so."

Chia-shan said, "Why?"

Replied Yuan-an, "Another house still has its own green mountains."

Chia-shan said, "If so, then my school will not collapse!"

The third example is of Zen sayings that go in and out of the realm of literature. As such there is a song by Zen Master "Lazy" Ts'an:

Immovable, without concerns, no changes;
Why should unconcern be the subject of discourse?
Just let the mind not be scattered or confused,
And there is no need to stop anything else.
The past is already past,
The future is still unaccounted:
Immovable, I sit unconcerned;
When has anyone ever called?
Those who seek exercises outside
Are all ignorant, sluggish clods.

They don't store a grain of provisions;
When there's food, all they know is to eat.
Worldly people, with many concerns,
Chase each other getting nowhere at all.
I don't wish to be born in heaven,
Nor do I love fields of blessings;
When hungry, I eat, when tired I sleep.
Foolish people laugh at me,
But the wise know what I'm about.
This is not ignorance or dullness.
The original substance is as it is;
I go when I want to go, stay when I want to stay.
I wear a single ragged patchwork robe,
With natural-born pants on my legs.
Many words and much talk
Turn out to be misleading;
If you want to liberate others,
Nothing is better than to liberate yourself for now.
Don't seek the real Buddha vainly;
The real Buddha cannot be seen.
Why should the subtle nature
And the pedestal of spirit need
To be trained and cultivated?
The mind is the mind with no concerns,
The face is the face born of woman:
The rock of ages may be moved,
But there is no change herein.
There is basically nothing to unconcern;
What's the need to read writings?
Strip away the root of person and ego,
And you will unconsciously accord with the
    meaning therein.
All kinds of exercises are not as good

As sleeping serenely in the woods.
When I raise my head, the sun is high;
Eating some rice, I start from the top.
Use effort to make effort,
And you become increasingly benighted.
Try to grasp it, and you don't get it;
Don't grasp, and it is spontaneously realized.
I have a saying
To cut off thought and forget objects;
It cannot be cleverly explained,
But only communicated by mind.
There is another saying,
No more than direct presentation,
Fine as a hairtip,
Vast beyond location,
Inherently complete and perfect,
Needing no work with loom and shuttle.
Worldly affairs are worrisome,
Not as good as the mountains and hills,
Green pines shading the sun,
Azure valley streams ever flowing,
The mountains and clouds as if tents,
The moon at night a hook.
Lying under the wisteria vines,
A rock for a pillow,
I do not pay court to the emperor,
So how could I envy the kings and lords?
Life and death are no worry;
Why be anxious at all anymore?
The moon in the water is formless;
I am always just peaceful.
Myriad things are all thus;
They are basically birthless themselves.

As I sit immovably unconcerned,
When spring comes the grass grows green of itself.

The fourth example is of Zen sayings that roam at
sport in the realm of romantic literature. The following
are illustrative verses of Zen Master Yu-hsien, who was
known as the Wine Immortal:

Green waters and red peach blossoms
Are met with wherever you go,
In the front streets and back alleys.
Everybody knows me, this one and that.
Knowing me, not knowing me:
Two fists, which one bigger?
Of the two, one is big:
Once it took and crushed the void,
Refined it like gold and restored it thus,
Took the polar mountain for a pillow as I lay.
The waves of the Yangtse River are deepest;
When travelers come here, all sink in thought.
Sometime if you come to where there are no waves,
Be as attentive as when there were waves:
Even a golden chalice has been known to spill,
Even a jade mountain has been reported to crumble;
Don't allow any further leakage or pressure.
If you chase the moonlight to take it back,
Buy expensive cinnabar to paint the moon,
When you figure it out, you've wasted effort.
Intoxicated, I lie beneath the shadow of green willow;
Getting up, I talk on about true suchness.
To a drunken man is carefully given this advice:
Don't lose the jewel in your clothes.
One six, two six, the thing's already enough;
One nine, two nine, I want to drink wine.

Stretching out my legs, I take a snooze;
When I wake up, the universe is still as before.
In the green trees in front of the gate there are no
   calling birds;
On the emerald moss at the foot of the yard there
   are some fallen flowers.
For a while I discuss this matter with the east wind;
To whom does this whole spectrum of spring color
   belong?
When autumn comes, the mountains are cold and
   the rivers frigid;
When spring arrives, the willows are green and
   the flowers red.
At a touch, action adapts to ten thousand changes;
In the river villages, it's misty and raining slightly.
Being, nonbeing, empty, not empty:
Sieves trying to catch the northwest wind.
Born in this world, human feelings
Involve how much love and hate:
I just want to drink some wine,
To fall in the alley and lie in the road.
After I die, I will again be born in this world;
I do not want to transcend to birth in the Pure Land.
What is the reason for this?
In the Pure Land of the West
There is no wine for sale.

PART V
The Heart and Goal of Zen

CHAPTER 13

The True Goal of Zen Study

Throughout the preceding discussions of the connections between Buddhism and Chinese history and culture, the simple introduction to the contents of Buddhism, and this last discussion of several important points about Zen, it can be generally understood that Zen is the mental reality of Buddhism, and that the main teaching of Buddhism lays emphasis on practical cultivation to seek realization, not on philosophical issues that are matters of purely theoretical discussion.

There is no question that the original Mahayana and Hinayana Buddhism, as well as the various individual schools of Buddhism founded in China, all had cultivation of meditation concentration as the backbone of their search for realization. The ultimate principles of the

teaching such as nirvana, essential emptiness, true suchness, and subtle being, as well as the fruits of attainment
of complete Buddhahood—such as the three bodies (of
reality, enjoyment, and emanation), the four knowledges
(to accomplish actions, of subtle observation, of essential
equality, and like a great round mirror), the six psychic
powers (clairvoyance, clairaudience, mental telepathy,
knowledge of former lives, the power of psychic travel,
and the power of ending contamination), the three com-
prehensions (of past lives, clairvoyance, and ending
contamination), as well as the ideas and realizations of
the conditional origination of essential emptiness and the
essential emptiness of conditional origination, the subtle
being of true emptiness and the true emptiness of subtle
being—these are all initially approached by way of meditation concentration to arrive at the experiential realization of *prajna*, after which they fulfill the complete fruit
of the Way, which is liberation.

After Zen was transmitted into China, even though
it evolved further into a Chinese-style school, it gradually
transformed the Buddhist teachings only in terms of
instructional method and linguistic expression, substitut-
ing colloquial language and popular literature to express
the lofty and profound principles of Buddhism. When it
came to the heart and goal of Zen, it still was not apart
from the original quest of Buddhism.

To put it another way, although the heart of Zen is
not meditation concentration, nevertheless it still has its
foundation in methods of cultivating meditation concentration to seek realization. Although the goal of Zen is
not the retirement of Hinayana Buddhism, which places
importance on leaving the world, avoiding society, and
escaping life and death, nevertheless it still involves a

process of sublimation of birth and death, seeking trans-mundane freedom of mind to enter the world to rescue sentient beings.

Even though the Zen masters of the T'ang, Sung, and later dynasties also adopted an instructional method that involved criticizing the Buddhas and reviling the patriarchs to break through religiosity fixated on blind faith, making proclamations such as the famous saying that Buddha is a "dry turd," nevertheless they professed that their goal was to arrive not at Buddhahood but sim-ply at a state of "ordinary people who have transcended convention," or "free Wayfarers without any concerns at all." In reality, these actions were all taken just to change things that were ordinarily imbued with excessive reli-gious coloring, such as epithets of Buddhas and bod-hisattvas, replacing them with concepts that were understandable to the common people; what the Zen masters called "transcending convention" and "free peo-ple" are not easily learned without serious effort.

Just think: if one is an ordinary person, and yet wants to transcend to a state beyond conventional com-parison even while in the midst of ordinary people; if this is just one human life, and yet one wants to "have no mind in things and no things in the mind" to attain the serene freedom that is "emptying what exists" and not "reifying what does not exist," how can this possibly be accomplished conveniently at one stroke? If people can really arrive at such a stage, even if you do not call them Buddhas but give them some other empty name, that nat-urally would mean nothing to them at all. It is like what Chuang-tzu says; be it an ox or a horse, let people call it whatever they may.

If we have comprehended the heart and goal of Zen

we can understand what the Zen masters of the T'ang and Sung dynasties meant when they spoke of comprehending life and death and seeking liberation. At the same time, the problems they raised, such as "what is the meaning of the coming of the Zen founder from India," and the function of their methods of initiatory guidance in learning Zen, such as "investigating a saying," can also become clear to the mind!

Now to go a step farther to clarify the evolution of this heart and goal of Zen, it is necessary to know the historical development of Chinese Buddhism. At the end of the Eastern Han dynasty, the vanguard of the transmission of Buddhism into China was not an infusion of academic theory. The prelude of the initial entry of Buddhism into China was, first, a manifestation of spiritual powers used by Indian monks, characterized by inconceivable phenomena beyond ordinary knowledge; and second, it was the instruction in practice of the Hinayana methods of cultivating meditation concentration.

Due to the fact that these two pioneering beginnings happened to coincide with the period of greatest flourishing of the activities of the Chinese Taoist methodologists, who had been inventing various kinds of methods of praxis since the Ch'in and Han dynasties in hopes of sublimating human life and entering into the realms of spiritual immortals, once they came in contact with the experiences of the meditation concentration and spiritual powers in Buddhism, the Taoists and Buddhists naturally observed and studied one another.

In extreme cases, where people became obsessed with meditation concentration in quest of spiritual powers, from the time of the Warring States era they made use of the practice of refining material elixirs for the philosopher's stone; compare this with the direction taken from the time of the Han dynasty toward the practice of refining vitality, spirit, and soul. What followed was the gradual importation of Buddhist thought and learning, which added a theoretical basis for full realization of the experiences cultivated in meditation concentration. That is why there were distinguished Buddhist monks and great worthies of the Wei, Chin, and North and South dynasties who successfully cultivated the various fruits of real experience. It was on this basis that the practical methods of meditation and contemplation used in the various schools of Buddhism, along with such teachings as the cessation and contemplation methods of the T'ien-t'ai school, were finally produced.

It is too bad that the usual run of Buddhist scholars do not dare to touch on these historical facts, because they themselves do not have any firsthand realization of the true experience of Buddhism. In extreme cases they retort that these are all empty words that have no relevance to Buddhist ideas at all. Such scholars have thereby caused the real meaning of Buddhist studies and the real goal of Zen studies to change their nature completely.

But then why did the Zen school from the Sui and T'ang dynasties onward reject meditation concentration in favor of the teaching of sudden enlightenment by seeing essence to realize Buddhahood? To answer this requires understanding of the task espoused and undertaken by the Zen school. We should know that the goal of the Zen school known as the special transmission beyond doctrine is to communicate the vision of true cultivation and genuine realization of the heart essence of Buddhism; it does not champion meditation concentration or psychic powers.

Since meditation concentration is a method common to Buddhism and all the religions of the world, all philosophies and branches of learning, and indeed even to the general run of ordinary people who cultivate calmness, it is not at all a special method originated by Buddhism alone. (A summary of the process of cultivation and realization of meditation concentration was given earlier in the section on the contents of Buddhism and will not be repeated here.) The realms of psychic or spiritual powers are also approached and entered psychologically and biologically, and then perfected by strict training in the methods of meditation concentration. This is a matter of laying hold of the instinctual potency of the essence and life of the body and mind of humans and all living beings, and employing it to the fullest extent of its capacity. So we know that even if the work of cultivating meditation concentration enables one to reach the realm of psychic powers, that is still not beyond the functioning of mind, will, and consciousness.

Meditation concentration and psychic powers are all creations of mind, realms of experience that can be reached through mind, will, and consciousness. If you gain some proficiency in these areas yet still cannot clearly understand what enables you to attain meditation concentration, what enables you to produce the functions of psychic powers, this mind that is the heart of the basic potency, then what is the condition of this state of yours in the ultimate sense? Where does it ultimately come from? Where is it ultimately going to? What sort of thing, in the ultimate sense, is its basic substance?

If one was accomplished in meditation concentration and psychic powers yet did not know this mind, would one not still be as before, an ignorant human being who does not know the ultimate nature of the universe and human life? That is why the *Lankavatara sutra* says that these states and experiences are nothing but disguises of consciousness itself. The sutra also clearly says, "Even if you attain the nine stages of concentration in the present, these are still things that are reflections of discrimination of phenomena as objects," thus summing up the case.

The Sung dynasty real human Chang Tzu-yang, who studied Zen through the Taoist school of spiritual immortalism, also said, "Even if you have a halo crowning your head, it is still a mirage; even if clouds arise under your feet, you are still not immortal!"

But to resume the discussion, if you are a real student of Buddhahood and a seeker of Zen, if you have not undergone strict training in meditation concentration, and have not even succeeded in mastering ordinary practices of mental hygiene that balance the mind and calm the mood, yet you make rash demands, perhaps even thinking yourself to have already attained the Zen Way of sudden enlightenment at a word, that is either stupidity or madness. I am afraid it is still far from the path of Zen! Even if people like this believe themselves to be really studying Zen, they are in my personal opinion the most benighted ignoramuses in the world, and all their decades of work seeking learning and realization have been wasted.

CHAPTER 14

The Process of Zen: Mental Work and Insight

To cut out the nonsense and get back to the real story, the heart and goal of Zen are as explained briefly above; as for the process of real Zen, if we reduce it to essentials there are two conditions, mental work and insight, which are like the two wings of a bird or the two wheels of a chariot—it is necessary to have both. I will now cite some examples of the great Zen masters of the early T'ang dynasty in relation to the mental work of practicing meditation concentration and the insight of seeing essence and awakening to the Way.

The Example of Ancestor Ma

Zen Master Tao-i of Kiangsi was surnamed Ma in lay life, so he is commonly called Ancestor Ma, or Great Master

Ma. During the K'ai-yuan era (713–741) of the T'ang dynasty, he was practicing concentration on Heng-yueh (also called Nan-yueh) in Hunan. At that time the Zen Master Huai-jang of Nan-yueh Mountain, who was one of the great disciples of the sixth patriarch and had attained the Dharma, knew that Ma was a great vessel of Buddhism. Therefore he went to ask him, "Great Worthy, [a term of respect used by Buddhists], what is your aim in sitting meditation?"

Ancestor Ma answered, "I want to become a Buddha."

Zen Master Huai-jang then took up a piece of tile and began rubbing it in front of the hermitage where Ma sat meditating every day. (Note that this is a Zen method of education.) One day Ancestor Ma asked the master, "Why are you rubbing the tile?" to which the master replied, "I am polishing it to make a mirror." Ancestor Ma then asked, "How can a tile be polished into a mirror?" The master answered, "Since polishing a tile does not make it a mirror, how can sitting meditation make one a Buddha?"

Hearing this, Ancestor Ma became doubtful, so he asked, "What would be right?" Master Huai-jang then explained, "It is like an ox pulling a cart: if the cart is not going, would it be right to hit the cart or to hit the ox?" (the cart symbolizes the body, the ox symbolizes the mind).

Having had this question posed to him, Ancestor Ma had no way to reply. It was not that he could not give an answer to this question; he was just in the process of making the principle of the metaphor clear and looking back into his own mind. The master also said, "Are you learning sitting meditation, or are you learning to be a

Buddha? If you are learning sitting meditation, meditation is not in sitting or reclining. If you are learning sitting Buddhahood, Buddhahood does not have a fixed form. Originally it is a teaching that does not dwell on anything, so there should be no attitude of grasping or rejection in relation to it. If you take sitting to be Buddhahood, that is equivalent to killing Buddha. If you cling to a fixed form of long sitting without moving to be Buddhism, you really do not understand the principle yet."

After listening to this, Ancestor Ma felt clear and refreshed, pleasantly elated, as if he had drunk some ambrosial elixir. He then bowed to the Zen master and again asked, "Then how should I apply my mind in order to attain formless *samadhi*?" (*Samadhi* is translated as "accurate reception.") The master answered, "Your study of the teaching of the mind ground is like planting seeds, while my explanation of the essentials of the Dharma is like the sky sending down rain and dew. Now that causal conditions are meet for you, you will naturally see the Way."

Ancestor Ma now asked, "If the Way has no visible form or appearance, how can it be seen?" Zen Master Huai-jang replied, "The spiritual eye of the mind ground itself can see the Way. Formless *samadhi* too is this very principle."

Then Ancestor Ma asked, "Does this have becoming and decay?" The Zen master answered, "If you see the Way in terms of becoming and decay, or in terms of assemblage and dissolution, then this is not the Way," after which he said in verse,

> *The mind ground contains all seeds;*
> *When there is moisture, all of them sprout.*

> *The flower of samadhi is formless;*
> *What decays, and what becomes?*

Hearing the master's instructions, Ancestor Ma gained access to enlightenment, and his mind soared to the freedom of liberation. After this he followed Great Master Huai-jang for nine years, making daily progress in penetrating the inner mysteries of the mental reality of Buddhism.

Now that I have told the story of the circumstances connected with the enlightenment of the great master Tao-i or Ancestor Ma, I trust it will be clear to everyone whether or not the teaching of Zen requires the key of meditation concentration work! But do not forget that it was through the activity of Great Master Ma that the culture of Chinese Zen in the T'ang dynasty finally began to work on a grand scale; he was an epoch-making man, not to be compared with ordinary shallow people. And even in his case, neither will it do to overlook the fact that he had certainly already gone through a long period of intense practice of meditation concentration before his enlightenment; only thus was he able to wake up to enlightenment suddenly on receiving the simple explanations of Great Master Huai-jang of Nan-yueh.

Even so, after his enlightenment, Ancestor Ma remained with his teacher for nine years, working for him, taking every opportunity to refine his realization of the Way to which he had awakened before he could penetrate the innermost mysteries. Let us ask ourselves if our capacities and virtues are superior to those of Great Master Ma. How can we arbitrarily say that the Zen of sudden enlightenment at a word is such an easy thing?

To sum up, learning and virtue are practical matters

and must be actually carried out and applied with true sincerity. This is especially true of Zen; it cannot be randomly sought or easily attained by frivolous conceits. I hope the youth of this generation will understand at a very deep level that nothing in the world can be done successfully with a hasty and careless attitude.

The Example of Master Fa-jung

Zen Master Fa-jung of Ox Head Mountain had studied all the Confucian classics and histories by the time he was nineteen years old. Then he read the Buddhist *Great Wisdom sutra* and realized a thorough understanding of true emptiness. All of a sudden, one day he lamented, "The worldly classics of the Confucians are not ultimate principles; the true vision of wisdom is a vehicle beyond the world." Then he went into seclusion on Mount Mao, where he entered into discipleship under a teacher and shaved his head to become a monk. Later he went to a cave on the northern crags of a temple on Ox Head Mountain called the Recondite Abode, where there occurred the marvel of birds bringing flowers to him.

During the Cheng-kuan era of the T'ang dynasty (627–649), the fourth patriarch of Zen, Great Master Tao-hsin, observed an atmospheric phenomenon from far off and realized an extraordinary person was living on that mountain, so he went by himself to try to find him. He inquired of the monks at a nearby temple, "Is there a man of the Way around here?" Though he was speaking to an ordained monk, his words were in effect the same as speaking to a lay person. He was actually upbraiding the monk for incompetence because monks are supposed to have left society for the express purpose of practicing the

Way. Thus we can see how straightforward and uncompromising the great Zen masters were, which is why they met with the loathing of worldlings wherever they went.

The monk asked, "What monk is not a man of the Way?" The fourth patriarch countered, "Ah! What one is a man of the Way?" to which the monk had no reply. Another monk then said, "A few miles deeper into the mountain there is someone called Lazy Jung, who does not rise when he sees people, and does not make any gesture of greeting. Might he not be a man of the Way?"

So the patriarch went into the mountain, and saw the master sitting there calmly in an upright position, paying no attention to him whatsoever. The patriarch asked, "What are you doing here?"

"Watching mind," replied the master.

The patriarch asked, "Who is watching? What is mind?" The master had no reply but got up, bowed, and inquired, "Where is your lofty abode, Great Worthy?"

The patriarch said, "I do not stay in any fixed place; sometimes I go east, sometimes west."

The master then asked, "Do you know Zen Master Tao-hsin?"

"Why do you ask about him?" the patriarch replied.

The master said, "For a long time I have been hearing of his virtue, and hope to get a chance to pay him a visit."

The patriarch said, "Zen Master Tao-hsin is this poor wayfarer, me."

The master then asked, "Why did you come here?"

The patriarch answered, "I came specially to visit you. Is there any place to stay?" The master pointed behind him and said there was a separate hut.

When the master led the patriarch to the hut, they

saw tigers and wolves surrounding it, so the patriarch raised his hands in a gesture of fright. The master inquired, "Does this still exist?" but the patriarch responded, "What is this?" The master then said nothing. Then the patriarch wrote the word Buddha on the rock where the master had been sitting. When the master saw it, he was startled; the patriarch asked him, "Does this still exist?" The master did not understand; he bowed his head and asked for an explanation of what is truly essential.

The patriarch explained, "The hundreds and thousands of gates to the truth are all ultimately in the mind; the subtle virtues as numerous as river sands are all in the source of mind. All aspects of discipline, concentration, wisdom, and manifestations of spiritual powers, are all inherently there, nowhere else but in your mind. All afflictions and obstructions caused by habit are originally void and null. All causes and effects are like dreams and hallucinations.

"There is no world to leave, no enlightenment to seek. Humans and nonhumans are equal in essence and character. The great Way is open and vast, beyond thought and reflection. You have now attained this truth and lack nothing more. You are no different from Buddha; there is no other teaching.

"Just let your mind be free: do not perform contemplative practices, and do not make your mind clear. Do not arouse greed or anger, do not embrace sorrow or worry. Flowing freely, unhindered, you are free in all ways, however you will. Not doing good, not doing evil, in all activities and circumstances, everything that meets your eyes is an inconceivable function of Buddhahood. It is blissful and sorrowless, so it is called Buddhahood."

The master said, "Granted that the mind is complete, what is Buddha, and what is mind?"

The patriarch answered, "If not for mind, there is no asking about Buddha; when asking about Buddha, it is not that it is not the mind."

The master then asked, "If I am not to perform contemplation practices, how should I quell my mind when objects arise?"

The patriarch therefore explained, "Objects are neither good nor bad; good and bad arise in the mind. If the mind does not insist on labeling, from where can deluded feelings arise? Once deluded feelings do not arise, the true mind is in charge of all knowledge. Just let your mind be independent and free, and do not try to quell it anymore; this is called the ever-present body of reality, and it has no change. I received the teaching of sudden enlightenment from Great Master Seng-ts'an, and now I hand it on to you. You now heard me clearly and truly; just live on this mountain, and later there will be five adepts who will carry on your original mission."

So the master lived on the mountain after this, and his teaching center became so populous as to be like that at Huang-mei, where the fifth patriarch of Zen taught. In the early 650s, when the followers were so numerous they lacked for provisions, the master went to the city, more than twenty-five miles away, to raise alms by preaching. Going in the morning, he would return at night with an enormous sack of grain on his back, which he gave to the congregation of three hundred students so they would not lack two meals a day. In three years a local governor invited the master to lecture on the *Great Wisdom sutra* at a temple, and huge crowds of people gathered to listen to him.

By this example of the circumstances connected with the enlightenment of Zen Master Fa-jung of Ox Head Mountain, it can be clearly understood that what Zen calls illumining the mind and seeing its essence has to do with the importance of insight. When Master Fa-jung was living alone on Ox Head Mountain practicing meditation concentration, he had already reached the realm where he forgot the scheming mind and was oblivious to things and self. That is why there occurred the marvel of birds bringing him flowers in their beaks.

This is similar to a story in the Taoist classic *Lieh-tzu* about someone living by the sea who palled around with a flock of seagulls every day: because he had no scheming mind, had no idea or thought of harming living creatures, and had already forgotten machinations to the point where he did not know the birds were birds and did not know he was himself, he and the gulls grew more familiar day by day.

Later, someone saw the man with the gulls and called out to him, telling him to take the opportunity to grab a few gulls and bring them over. When the man heard this, it stirred his mechanical mind, and he prepared to grab a gull. But once the birds saw him in this state, they immediately flew away before he could catch them.

Thus it is obvious that Master Fa-jung's practice of meditation concentration had not only reached the realm where one forgets machinations and the self, but also still had within it the virtue of mercy and love toward the life of beings as well as profoundly deep achievement in meditation concentration. That is why the fourth patriarch Tao-hsin told him that he already had everything except an awakening.

But even after he awakened to the Way, he still worked hard for the sake of others. For a large congregation of ordinary students, he personally went down the mountain to preach for alms, coming back with a load of rice to feed everyone. No longer would he have birds bringing flowers in their beaks, or have ghosts and spirits send rice to protect the Dharma! This principle, this key, is one that should be studied above all by people who are obsessed with occultism; for the moment we will refrain from adding explanations for them.

Next, after the fourth patriarch Tao-hsin arrived on Ox Head Mountain, he saw some tigers and wolves; he threw up his hands and put on an expression of fright. Because of this, Master Fa-jung gave rise to doubt and asked him, "Do you still have the kind of psychology that is afraid of tigers and wolves?" The fourth patriarch immediately asked him back, "What is this that can become afraid?" If Fa-jung replied that it is mind, where is the mind? And what is it like? Where does it come from? Where does it go? Does it exist after death? There must be a whole string of questions to go on pursuing. But Master Fa-jung did not go on, and the fourth patriarch said no more.

Now the fourth patriarch wanted to seize the opportunity to create a situation in which he could give him some education, so he wrote the word Buddha on the rock where Fa-jung usually sat and then sat down himself. To a sincerely pious Buddhist like Fa-jung, who left home to study Buddhism, this would have seemed like a truly blasphemous act, so he became upset and was very suspicious of this man who called himself the fourth patriarch of Zen.

The fourth patriarch had already figured that the

master would react like that, so he immediately asked, "Do you still have the mentality that gets upset because of worshiping images without knowing where the real Buddha is?" The patriarch was taking the opportunity to educate the master, to get him to understand that the mentality of fear about which Fa-jung had asked, and the mentality of being upset about which the patriarch was asking now, are just different aspects of the functioning of this mind. Whether it be joy, anger, sadness, happiness, or any sort of psychological or physiological change, all are just activities of the mind. If you do not clearly understand the substance and characteristics of the fundamental source of the nature of this mind, then whatever you may learn is all just seeking outside of mind; it has no truth in it, since it is just dependent functioning of mind according to changes in the physical environment.

In this way Fa-jung realized his own mistake, and then asked the fourth patriarch to teach him. Only thus did he draw out a long discourse on principles from the patriarch, who clearly told him the essential methods of cultivating the mind ground. (The original document is quoted above; please forgive me for not deeming it necessary to add a lot of explanatory notes. All you have to do is read it carefully, and it should naturally become clear to you. Too much talk, on the other hand, would be like drawing legs on a picture of a snake.)

But even after this the fourth patriarch still told Master Fa-jung to stay in the mountains and practice quietly. Only after going through a long period of refinement did the master come down from the mountain with a mind transcending things to work for the actualization of his teaching mission for the benefit of the people of the world. No longer was he "Lazy Jung." All that hardship and toil, all the effort and labor, he did entirely for the sake of other people.

By this it can be known that if we young people of today, who were born in a time of great difficulty for the country and the world, want to bear the responsibility for taking care of our families, governing our nations, and bringing peace to the world, unless we are highly cultivated and work in the world with transmundane hearts, we will be stymied by present realities and become narrow-minded and afflicted with selfishness. Please excuse me for saying this; it is not up to me to preach, but when I came to this point in my talk these admonitions seemed to slip right out of my mouth!

The Example of Master Ch'ang-ch'ing Hui-leng

Zen Master Ch'ang-ch'ing Hui-leng went back and forth for twenty years between Hsueh-feng and Hsuan-sha, two great Zen masters. Over this period of time he wore out seven cushions sitting in meditation. Nevertheless he still did not understand Zen. Then one day when he rolled up a bamboo blind, he suddenly had a great awakening. He composed a verse saying,

> *What a difference! What a difference!*
> *Rolling up the blind, I see the whole world.*
> *If anyone asks me what religion I understand,*
> *I will raise my whisk and directly strike.*

Hsueh-feng said to Hsuan-sha, "He has penetrated through." "Not yet," replied Hsuan-sha, "This is a product of ideational consciousness. He must be tested again."

That evening, when the community of monks came up to greet the Zen master, Hsueh-feng said to Ch'ang-ch'ing,

"Hsuan-sha does not agree with you yet; if you really have true enlightenment, bring it out to the assembly." So Ch'ang-ch'ing composed another verse, saying,

> *In myriad forms one body's revealed alone;*
> *Only when people realize it themselves is it their own.*
> *In the past I searched by mistake on the road;*
> *Today I look on it as ice within fire.*

Hsueh-feng looked at Hsuan-sha and said, "You can't consider this a product of ideational consciousness any more, can you?"

The Example of Master Ling-yun Chih-ch'in and Peach Blossoms

Zen Master Ling-yun Chih-ch'in studied with Zen Master Kuei-shan. He awakened to the Way on seeing peach blossoms, and composed a verse saying,

> *For the last thirty years I've looked for a*
> * swordsman;*
> *How many times have the leaves fallen and new*
> * twigs sprouted?*
> *Ever since seeing the peach blossoms once,*
> *To this day I no longer doubt.*

Upon reading this verse, Kuei-shan questioned Ling-yun's enlightenment and found that it tallied. Kuei-shan said, "When you attain enlightenment through conditions, you never backslide or lose it. Best keep it secure yourself."

From the third and fourth examples, it can be seen that Zen enlightenment places emphasis on the work of cultivating and realizing meditation concentration as well as on the insight to perceive the Way. Zen Master Ch'ang-ch'ing Hui-leng sat for twenty years, wearing out seven cushions, and still did not understand Zen; after his enlightenment, he again went through strict testing by the Great Masters Hsueh-feng and Hsuan-sha before he really got it right. People who study Zen today say they have attained enlightenment without having even sat through a single grass mat, but I'm afraid it is not quite so easy.

Also, consider the example of Master Ling-yun awakening to the Way on seeing peach blossoms; it looks very relaxed and elegant, and indeed rich in literary ambience, but you must not by any means forget the hard work to which he referred when he said, "For the last thirty years I've looked for a swordsman"! If you think that the ancients were immediately enlightened with consummate ease upon seeing peach blossoms or plum flowers, consider how many fine flowers you have seen in the course of your lives; why are you not yet enlightened?

Even if the story were interpreted to mean that once Ling-yun saw the peach blossoms he awoke to the principle of the activity of living potential, and this counts as Zen, since you have seen people eating food, wherein there is even more of the function of the activity of living potential, you should have been enlightened long ago. For example, Newton discovered an earth-shaking rule of science on seeing an apple fall to the ground, but just think of how many people past and present have eaten apples every day without discovering anything new. So in this way it can be known that awakening to the Way on seeing peach blossoms is not within your purview!

Aside from these examples, people often bring up another Zen story about seeing that the mountains are not mountains, seeing that the rivers are not rivers, and seeing the mountains and seeing the rivers; so I might as well include a discussion of it here. This story comes from a statement given in a formal lecture by Zen Master Wei-cheng, who said, "Thirty years ago, before I had studied Zen, I saw the mountains were mountains and the rivers were rivers. Later, when I had personally seen a Zen teacher and had attained initiatory experience, I saw that the mountains are not mountains and the rivers are not rivers. But now that I have attained peace, I see the mountains simply as mountains, and see the rivers simply as rivers. Tell me, everyone, are these three views the same or different? If anyone can distinguish the black from the white, I will admit that you have seen me in person."

Because this story is part of traditional Zen lore, students of later generations, including people all over the world today, have taken it as a handle on Zen study. Some people say it represents the so-called three barriers of Zen. Others say that it is necessary to reach the point at which you see that mountains are not mountains and rivers are not rivers, and then turn around again to arrive at seeing mountains as mountains and rivers as rivers again; this they identify as the realm of great penetration and great enlightenment. In reality, these explanations are ultimately just impressionistic talk; these views may seem to be correct, but they are not.

First of all, it is necessary to understand clearly that this talk by Zen Master Wei-cheng is about his own personal experience in practice. When it comes to the matter of whether Master Wei-cheng had actually attained great penetration and great enlightenment himself, you first of all cannot invent some fabrication and make up a subjective determination of the issue on his behalf.

His first stage, where he says he saw mountains as

mountains and rivers as rivers, of course, represents the state of anyone before studying the Zen Way. Everyone is like this, seeing the mountains, rivers, and earth, the various human and natural environments in the physical world clearly and distinctly; this does not require any special interpretation.

For the second stage, where he said he saw mountains are not mountains and rivers are not rivers, it is one hundred percent certain that this is a state achieved through the actual application of meditation concentration work. If one has genuinely practiced meditation concentration work and the method and process of cultivation realization, and if one's inner and outer physical and mental application and conduct have not gone astray in any way, then eventually this should cause the physical and mental temperament and constitution to undergo a great change. The eyes will be full of spiritual light, the spirit will solidify, the energy will mass, and the material word seen by the eyes, the mountains, rivers, land, and so on will naturally seem as though one is in a waking dream, like images of light reflected in water. One will feel that everything in this material world is all dreamlike, illusory existence, totally unreal; and one will also see people as like mechanical robots.

Many people who reach this stage, whether they are studying Zen or practicing Taoism, thereupon assume it is the true Way, but really this sort of state has nothing to do with the Way. This happens because of long immersion of the body and mind in quiet concentration, resulting in diminution of psychological and biological instincts, and repletion with vital energy that causes the brain and nervous system to undergo a change resembling electrical charging, so one sees the phenomena before one as ephemeral and has no feeling of reality. This is similar to the scattering of vision experienced when the body is depleted and weakened after a serious illness, or when one is about to die. Of course, this phenomenon associated with sickness and dying does not itself represent the state of people practicing meditation concentration who see mountains and rivers as not being mountains and rivers: it is just a way of making a comparison. One is due to illness or dying; one arises from being filled with the living power of life; so they are not exactly the same.

But you must not forget that this kind of phenomenon is just a different sensation of the biological organs; what enables you to produce such feelings and cognition is still the function of your consciousness and thought. If you assume that seeing mountains as not being mountains and seeing rivers as not being rivers is a good phenomenon reflecting practice of Zen or Tao, that is still mediocre; if so, then you might as well take a hallucinogenic pill or a moderate dose of tranquilizers, for would that not cause a similar marvel? Can you say this is the Way?

So many people who study Zen and lecture on Zen today, both in China and the rest of the world, often bring up this issue. I cannot but add some explanation to the matter so that practitioners avoid making the mistake of entering into byways and ruining the useful physical body.

Coming to Zen Master Wei-cheng's third stage of seeing the mountains as mountains again and seeing the rivers as rivers again of course represents a Zen state where he had advanced a step farther, so he said of himself that he had attained peace. If you just go by these remarks and assume that this is great penetration and great enlightenment, then you might as well relax and go to sleep, waking up to see that mountains are still mountains and rivers are still rivers. Would this not be more direct and enjoyable?

Therefore it is really not easy at all to read the classics and stories of Zen; we should not by any means become confused by fragmentary interpretations. It is essential to seek personal experience of realization; only then do you know the ultimate. If we were to take this one story, which only points to a process of practice, and augment it so that it would be perfectly complete, we would have to cite the saying of T'ang dynasty Zen Master Nan-ch'uan, "When people today see this flower, it is like a dream," to be able to approach the final Zen work of letting go. In sum, this story only refers to the mental work involved in Zen; it is not completely relevant to the insight of enlightenment.

CHAPTER 15

Nirvana and the Aim of Zen

The message of Zen is as Shakyamuni Buddha himself announced at the meeting on Spiritual Mountain when he twirled the flower, "I have the treasury of the eye of true teaching, the ineffable mind of nirvana, the true form that has no form, a subtle teaching that does not set up written words but is specially transmitted outside of doctrine." So we know that, in the context of Chinese Buddhism, Zen was originally a sect developed by taking up the message of Shakyamuni Buddha that was specially transmitted outside of doctrine and did not set up written words. Clearly there is something special about Zen that is different from the manner in which the other schools of Buddhism transmitted and received Buddhist studies.

If you want to study Zen, first you should obtain a clear understanding of the ultimate point of the teachings that Shakyamuni Buddha expounded over the forty–nine years of his career. In general, we all know that the scriptures and classics on the teachings he left are comprised of three treasuries and twelve parts. The three treasuries (or baskets) are the sutras, scriptural discourses; the Vinaya, or rules of conduct; and the Abhidharma, or analytic treatises on the Dharmas of the sutras. The twelve parts refer to a division of the whole Buddhist canon into twelve categories based on the thirty-third book of the *Ta Chih Tu Lun,* or *Treatise on the Perfection of Great Wisdom,* which names them as follows: first, sutras; second, recapitulatory verses; third, chants; fourth, chains of events; fifth, past deeds; sixth, past lives; seventh, Abhidharma, which in this case translates as unprecedented or incomparable teachings; eighth, parables; ninth, discussions and debates; tenth, extemporaneous talks; eleventh, extension and expansion of the teaching; and twelfth, predictions. The sutras, recapitulatory verses, and chants are literary forms of scripture; the other nine categories refer to different matters that come up in the scriptures.

Of course, however, the Buddhist canon includes both Mahayana and Hinayana teachings, which are different only with respect to the relative depth of their transmissions, in terms of method and degree. The resulting state and the aim they seek to attain, liberation and nirvana, are not two different aims. In other words, even if nirvana does have differences in the Mahayana and Hinayana, the Mahayana nirvana without remaining dependence and the Hinayana nirvana with remaining dependence clearly are different in depth of stage and degree as to the highest vision of realization sought and the ultimate theoretical principle, but they are the same in their goal of proceeding toward nirvana.

Nirvana is a Buddhist term that represents the total being of the body and mind of the life of all things and all creatures in the universe, when it is in a state before any impulses have stirred, in the condition of original quiescence when not a single thought of body (physiological phenomena) or mind (psychological conditions) has arisen. It is silent and unmoving, a stage transcending the metaphysical; so in Buddhism it is also called the state of extinction to describe this realm and its absoluteness, formlessness, freedom from agitation, and absence of objects. But nirvana is also called the great awakening of complete illumination and purity to bring out the fact that its effective potential is not empty stillness like the extinction of death.

The form of nirvana is formless; this is its real form. That is why it transcends thought and consciousness. It is a subtle teaching that cannot be completely expressed in words, writings, or theories. This is the one true eye in the total Buddhist teaching, and it is the authentic goal embraced by all Buddhist doctrines. So if we are looking for an initiatory method of realizing nirvana, speaking in human terms, there is no special way other than to start from this present body and mind. But speaking in terms of the basic efficacy of this body and mind, biological and psychological functions are all capacities of the ineffable mind of nirvana. The final and highest goal of human life in the universe as sought by all religion, philosophy, and science of all times and all places is precisely the quest for the realization of this.

If we were temporarily to borrow philosophical terminology, it is the metaphysical essence of all things in the universe and the nature and destiny of human life. Of course, from that standpoint, from that angle, it is called

Buddha, or Heaven, or Lord, or God, or Spirit, or the Way, or Being, or Mind. It is also given various descriptions to which various names and epithets may or may not be applied; yet all, without exception, refer to this.

When it puts on the outer clothing of religion, it is apotheosized; when it takes on the form of philosophy, it turns into the ideal. When it climbs up onto the throne of science, it turns into efficacy. But no matter how you explain it or interpret it, ultimately that explanation or interpretation is not what it is really and truly like. That is because as soon as it falls into the function of speech and language, it is revolving around within the limited domain of ideational consciousness, thinking and imagining. Since the intellectual functions of the speech and language produced by thinking and imagining of ideational consciousness are themselves interdependent, relative, and changing in their formation, so they are not absolute and unchanging truths.

When Shakyamuni Buddha held up a flower in front of the assembly at Spiritual Mountain, the whole crowd remained silent, saying nothing, not knowing where the message was. Only the honorable Kasyapa broke into a smile, and Shakyamuni then said he had this teaching, "the treasury of the eye of true teaching, the ineffable mind of nirvana, the true form without form, the subtle teaching that does not insist on literary expression but is specially transmitted outside of doctrine, transmitted to Kasyapa." This became the story of the first transmission of Zen outside of doctrine.

In actual reality, "doctrine" means "principle," and the special transmission outside of doctrine is the identity of principle and fact, which means that fact and principle merge, resulting in the fruit of direct attainment. Flowers bloom, flowers fall: everything is the ineffable mind of nirvana, the marvelous free-living function of natural potential. Who holds up the flower? Who is the flower? Who can hold it up? Is what is held up a flower? Is it not a flower? Is the flower smiling? Is Kasyapa smiling? Who is it that smiles? Is Kasyapa smiling at the flower? Or is he smiling at the needlessness of the Buddha's gesture of holding up the flower? Is holding up a flower holding up a flower? Is smiling smiling? Is there much of an atmosphere here of "eagles soaring in the heavens, fish leaping in the depths"? Or is it a realm of "gazing over the bend in the river, where the bamboos grow thick"? There are a lot of problems, or there may be no problem at all: this is really a most excellent strategic approach to the issue, but it is free spirited and down to earth.

Beginning with Shakyamuni Buddha holding up the flower and Kasyapa breaking into a smile, the pressure of the grandeur and solemnity of the Buddha's past sermons transmitting mind was swept away. It was as if someone had had to travel over a thousand mountains and cross ten thousand rivers in search of a place to lodge, making a seemingly interminable journey where "the mountains and rivers go on and on, and it seems there is no road," and then suddenly broke through a thin but blinding mist to find the way before him even and level, the grasses growing and the orioles flying about, the birds calling and the flowers blooming—endless living potential greeting his mind and eyes. Now he had found the real countenance of the life of body and mind, nature and destiny, and with a special sense of understanding he simply smiled at it.

This is the savor of the experience that is, as Great Master Hsuan–tsang described, "Like when someone drinks water; he knows for himself if it is cool or warm." It cannot even be imagined by anyone who has not had the experience; this is truly the ineffable mind of nirvana, the subtle teaching that is specially transmitted outside of doctrine, which cannot be reached by intellectual conceptions.

Having come to China, after Bodhidharma's direct pointing to the human mind to see its essence and attain Buddhahood, the second patriarch Hui-k'e was able to find a way to peace of mind with but a few words of instruction, and over a period of somewhat more than a century it was transmitted five times until it reached the sixth patriarch Hui-neng, who initiated the full scale development of the T'ang dynasty Zen school. After this the Zen method of teaching, such as that of Master Ma-tsu Tao-i and his successors, was very much in the manner of Shakyamuni Buddha's raising the flower and Kasyapa's smiling. It might be raising the eyebrows and winking, or a blow of the cane or a shout, or holding up a single finger, or puffing on the nap of a blanket, or awakening to the Way on seeing peach blossoms, and penetrating enlightenment on hearing the sound of a bell. Most of the Zen masters penetrated enlightenment and reached the most extraordinary and recondite of ineffable truths in the course of ordinary daily affairs, within the goings on of the most normal and down-to-earth events. The teaching that speaks of sudden enlightenment at a word, understanding mind, seeing its essence, and becoming a Buddha on the spot is just this simple and handy.

However, the Zen school is called the heart of Buddhism: if its teaching of special transmission outside of doctrine is this simple, does that possibly mean that the teachings spoken by Shakyamuni over his lifetime were all a useless waste? And is the same true of the efforts of the Indian and Chinese patriarchs, eminent monks, and great worthies in their studies of mastering conduct, cultivating concentration, and realizing wisdom, investigating "doctrines, principles, practices, and results" in search of "faith, understanding, application, and realization" to arrive at "hearing, thinking, cultivation, and wisdom"? Were they all deceptive amusements?

In reality they were not. What Zen calls the special transmission outside of doctrine simply refers to the method of transmission of the entire range of theory and practice for true realization. It does not mean that there is a secret transmission of the mind sealed apart from the principles of the doctrines of the teaching. It goes without saying that the true reality of the doctrines within Buddhism, as well as the special transmission outside of doctrine, is in any case concerned with seeking realization of the root source of the essence and life of body and mind. That is what is called the fruition of nirvana, in which the essence of mind is inherently perfect and complete. Whenever the doctrines of the teaching talk about mind and its essential nature, they call it true suchness, or the nature of the matrix of realization of suchness, or equivalent terms, all of which simply refer to this.

In other words, the mind referred to by what Buddhism calls the ineffable mind of nirvana is not the mind that functions in a discriminatory manner through thought based on intellectual consciousness imbued with the ideas of person and ego. What is meant by mind, nature, or essence in Buddhism refers to the ineffable mind that has the same root as the universe and is one body with all things, the ineffable mind that is the totality of true suchness.

When people in ancient times talked about the inner reality of Buddhahood, and translated Buddhist writings because there was no applicable vocabulary, they tended to use the ordinary word "mind" to represent the heart of the ontological unity of all things and beings in the universe. They also used "mind" to represent mind in the psychological sense of the discriminatory function of intellectual consciousness and thought. This caused later students of Buddhism to mistake the thinking mind of ideational consciousness for the inner absorption of the ineffable mind of nirvana spoken of by the Buddha, but there is a very great difference between them.

Of course, it cannot be denied that this thinking mind of ideational consciousness is none other than one type of function of the subtle mind of true suchness, in which all things and beings in the universe, mental and material, are one suchness. Because of this, as the tradition of Zen flowed through the late T'ang dynasties, the Five dynasties, and the Sung and Yuan dynasties, the teaching eventually became degenerate, gradually becoming tangled and confused, so that many people confused the subtle mind of true suchness with the function of ideational consciousness and thought patterns. They looked on this mind of psychological patterns and ideational consciousness as the way of the mind ground taught in Zen. Among the degeneracies, the greatest changes developed along two main pathways.

The first of these was the formulation of the fashion of Zen study characteristic of the Sung and Yuan dynasties and thereafter. It took the original teaching of direct pointing to the human mind to see its essence and attain Buddhahood, reamalgamated it with the contemplations of Hinayana meditation, and drew on meditation concentrations based on the cultivation of *dhyana* contemplation. It united these into one and considered the search for realization of single-minded concentration, or a state of undisturbed stillness, to be the initial work of Zen. This produced the teaching methods of Zen such as "investigating a *hua-t'ou*," and "doing *kung-fu*," which are based on quiet sitting in meditation concentration, or considering the practice of clarifying the mind with silent awareness (absorption in silence) as itself the principle of Zen.

Second was the development of neo-Confucianism in the Sung dynasty, which was a Buddhist-influenced form of Confucianism. It was based on the idea that the essence of mind is inherently complete and perfect. It was understood that even as one practices detachment from the world and transcendence of conventions as well as entering into the world to help living beings, actually carrying out the Mahayana bodhisattva path of saving the world, the essence of mind itself fundamentally does not increase or decrease, is not defiled or pure. Here the doctrines of Confucianism and Buddhism interacted and combined, with the inclination toward involvement in the world forming the Sung dynasty school of neo-Confucianism.

Now let me explain a little about the main trends of these two courses of development in the Zen schools during and after the Sung and Yuan dynasties.

CHAPTER 16

On the Zen Fashion of Emphasizing
Concentration on a Word or Saying During and
After the Sung and Yuan Dynasties

With the arising and flourishing of the five sects of Zen in the T'ang and Five dynasties, Chinese Zen changed from the original method of pointing directly to the human mind to see its essence and attain Buddhahood, to dispensing teaching according to the situation. Thus it became an instructional method of pointing to things to communicate mind in the midst of ordinary situations and surroundings of the ordinary reality of the immediate present. After that, coming to the end of the Sung dynasty and the beginning of the Yuan dynasty, overtaken by accumulating deterioration, many followers started clinging to the state of mind and body in the immediate present, considering this the Zen potency and thus falling into clichés. They did not know the caveat, as Zen Master Chia-shan explained, that "There is no objective reality in the immediate present; the idea is in the immediate present. This is not the phenomena of the immediate present; it is not within reach of ear or eye."

Due to this, Zen teachers with enlightened perceptions such as Ta-hui Tsung-kao, Kao-feng Yuan-miao, and Chung-feng Ming-pen changed the method again and now extolled the approach of investigating a *hua-t'ou* or a word. From then on, through the Yuan, Ming, and Ch'ing dynasties and thereafter, it generally became customary to think of Zen practice in terms of "investigating a word," "arousing a feeling of doubt," and "passing through three barriers," and to regard these as the Zen teaching of nonduality.

Eventually this caused Zen to degenerate in practical terms, taking to silent awareness (submerging thought in still silence) or a state of stillness as the one and only method. As the ancients said, "Trying to knock at the gate of Zen, traveling to groups all over the place, has deluded so many young people!" "Piling up snow for provisions, polishing bricks to make tiles, how many have reached old age without accomplishing anything!" "At the precipice of thoughtlessness, under the tree without shadows, who can recognize the spring dawn at the call of the partridge?" These sayings refer to the results of this deterioration in Zen.

Now I will give a general introduction and brief discussion about such methods as "investigating a saying" to help everyone understand the reasons why latter-day Zen went through the changes that brought it to its present degenerate state.

On the Relationship Between Investigating a *Hua-t'ou*, the Practice of Cessation and Contemplation, and *Dhyana*

A *hua-t'ou*, which literally means a word or a saying, is in modern terminology equivalent, in its general conceptual meaning, to a problem or question. However, it still is of a different character because when we come up with a problem or question in our minds, we can use our brains to ponder, examine, investigate, associate, hypothesize, and analyze endlessly until we come to the point at which we feel we have reached an answer and consider ourselves satisfied. Or if we can see fundamentally no way to resolve it, we can set it aside, or else shift into another domain of thought where it turns into an emotion, a state of joy, anger, sadness, or happiness.

A *hua-t'ou* is not like this. It is a question or problem, but when we add the word "investigate" to make the expression "investigate a *hua-t'ou*," it has a different function from an ordinary question about something doubtful. A *hua-t'ou* is of course a problem, but the ancients called it a word or a saying because they referred to all the ratiocinative functions of conscious thinking and its relation to language as a "saying." Therefore, whenever conscious thought begins to operate, that is the start of a saying. But where does any saying, which is a motivating impulse at the time of the initial stirring of thought, come from? And after it has passed, where does it go? This kind of reflection stirring thought, along with the issue of where the question itself comes from and where it goes, is one big question.

If you want to find the beginning of this stirring of thought to ponder a question, that is the *hua-t'ou*. It is the beginning of a statement, of a question; "investigating a *hua-t'ou*" is thus a way of investigating the source and basis of this statement. In this context, the word "investigation" includes the combined functions of reflection, comprehension, examination, investigation, observation, meditation, and so on.

The first person in ancient China to bring up this method of practice was Wei Po-yang of the Eastern Han dynasty, who used this method of "investigation" in the process of cultivating, understanding, and awakening to the Tao. Whether or not the Zen schools of the T'ang and Sung dynasties and thereafter borrowed it from him, or whether they just happened to coincide, is a question that one dare not decide arbitrarily, due to lack of documented data.

After the Zen school had formulated the method of investigation, the Zen schools of the Ming and Ch'ing dynasties took it a step farther; they often took the expression "investigate a saying" and called it "gazing on a saying," thus inclining solely to the method of contemplative observation and quiet watching, turning it into the function of observing the mind and watching over thoughts.

Watching Thoughts

If we study the methods of Zen practice and realization, or what is usually called Zen work, and if we study the actual practical methods of the various schools of Buddhism, such as the stopping and seeing practices of the T'ien-t'ai school, the Buddha remembrance practice of the Pure Land school, and the visualization practices of the Esoteric school, we should have some understanding of the words "thought" and "watching thought" as well as the meaning and function of thought.

"Thought" refers to the psychological activity of thinking consciousness as well as the function of emotions and physiologically ingrained sensations, all of which are summed up in the word. For example, when the vicious habit of eating or smoking opium was popular near the end of the Ch'ing dynasty, in one region of eastern China it was said of opium addicts that when their craving arose, their "thought" had come.

If we start categorizing the thoughts of human life precisely, we find that they are extremely numerous. There are the emotions of joy, anger, sadness, and happiness, as well as the three kinds of inferior roots in the basis of the psyche as explained in Buddhism, namely, greed, anger, and folly (murder, thievery, and licentiousness). Then there are the eighty-eight binding compulsions analyzed in the Hinayana school of Abhidharma, the fifty-three mental elements spoken of in the Mahayana school of Vijnanavada, the contents of the eight consciousnesses, and so on. All of these are covered by the single general word "thought."

The method of "watching over thought" (more simply expressed as "watching thought") used in Zen schools since the Ming and Ch'ing dynasties is a matter of observing the functions of the mind. I have already talked in a general way about the method of observing the functions of mind as they arise and disappear, explaining it by the formula of dividing them into past, present, and future, so I need not repeat that discussion. Other than this, using the method of "investigating a saying," "watching a saying," or "gazing at a saying" to study Zen is like the teaching on practicing stopping and seeing (cessation and contemplation): first one does preparatory practices to tune the body (physiological adjustments) and the breathing (modulation of the respiration), after which one comes to clarifying the mind and meditating quietly. The first steps to bring the mind to a state of unified concentration without distraction belong to the domain of stopping thoughts, which is prior to the practice of contemplation in stopping and seeing. Thus progressing in an orderly manner, this is the very same process as the four meditations and eight concentrations described earlier.

From keeping the mind on one point to attain a state of quiet cessation and complete single-mindedness, the practitioner goes on to initiate contemplative observation, examining the traces of the goings and comings of the thoughts in the mind, or searching for an answer to a *hua-t'ou.* This phase of practice belongs to the realm of contemplative exercise, similar to the T'ien-t'ai method of cultivation known as the three kinds of stopping (cessation) and three kinds of seeing (contemplation). These are generally the same, with but a slight difference in purpose.

Coming to the visualization practice of the Esoteric school of Buddhism, and the old native Chinese Taoist practice of refining spirit, which is the practice and method referred to by the expressions "purifying rectitude to enter the spiritual" and "purifying thought to enter the spiritual," they are just about the same, except for differences in purpose and dissimilarities in format. That is why Taoist charms and spells of later times have numerous similarities with the spells of Esoteric Buddhism.

Investigating a *Hua-t'ou*

No matter how the slogan "directly pointing to the human mind to see its essence and attain Buddhahood" was espoused in the "investigating Zen" and "investigating a *hua-t'ou*" practiced in Zen schools since Ming and Ch'ing times, they were clearly very different from T'ang and Sung dynasty Zen in terms of instructional method and mode of format. The later Zen schools had already turned around and run back into the combined domain of meditational contemplations of primitive Hinayana Buddhism, *dhyana* (meditation concentration, cultivation of contemplation), stopping and seeing, visualization, and the "purification of thought" of the higher grade of spiritual alchemy practiced by the orthodox Taoists of China. Therefore, for most of the real Zen students, rather than say they were members of the Zen school, it would be more appropriate to say that they were studying the Tao, or the Way.

But are "investigating a *hua-t'ou* and "purifying thought to enter the spiritual" really completely the same? Not so, not so! What is different about investigating a *hua-t'ou* is that, within the state of quiet stillness in meditation concentration, it contains a question that everyone of every time and every place has to resolve and yet cannot in fact actually answer. If in the process of progressive practice of investigating meditation one manages to reach the necessary states and stages of the four meditations and eight concentrations, this is called doing Zen work; and if in this state of Zen meditation work one finds an opening and clarification of wisdom and knowledge, so that one clearly awakens to realization of the basis of this great question, this is called the state of insight at which one opens up in enlightenment.

In sum, vision without work is the random imagination of misguided intellect; work without insight is externalist meditation, or the meditation of the ordinary person, which seeks something outside of mind. Then what *hua-t'ou* do they investigate in the state of meditation concentration? To give a brief and simplified introduction, *hua-t'ou* can be divided into two kinds: those that have logical meaning, and those that have no logical meaning.

Examples of *hua-t'ou* that have logical meaning are as follows: Where do we come from when we are born? Where do we go when we die? Who is it that remembers Buddha? Who is it who thinks? What is the mind? And so on. Then there is the one most favored by Zen Master Ta-hui Tsung-kao of the Southern Sung dynasty: Buddha said that all sentient beings have Buddha nature; so when a monk asked master Chao-chou if a dog has Buddha nature or not, why did Chao-chou say "no"? What is the principle? He even went to the extreme of teaching people that it was enough just to investigate the single word "no," inquiring into the question of what its principle is.

The following are examples of *hua-t'ou* without logical meaning: What is Buddha?—The cypress tree in the yard; What is Buddha?—Three pounds of flax; What is Buddha?—A dry turd, and so on.

In between those that have logical meaning and those that have no logical meaning are those that are what is usually referred to as "investigating a *kung-an*," which take historical accounts of the enlightenment of the ancients, stories of how they studied and awakened, as well as sayings from the dialogues of teachers and students, and make them into mirrors, bringing out what is essential in them to use to investigate one's own question. That is called investigating a *kung-an* or public case.

The practice of investigating a *hua-t'ou* used in the Zen schools since the Yuan and Ming dynasties includes these functions, so it is quite different from the practical operations of specialization in meditation concentration, cessation and contemplation, visualization, or the Taoist practice of "purifying thought to enter the spiritual."

CHAPTER 17

The Doctrine of the Three Barriers
and the Realm of Zen Investigative Meditation
Since the Yuan and Ming Dynasties

In the Zen schools during and after the Sung and
Yuan dynasties, due to the popularity of the method
of investigating a *hua-t'ou* and the diffusion of the
monastic system of the practicing Zen communes, the
meditation halls in the great Zen organizations and Zen
cloisters throughout the land had equivalent standards
everywhere. Thus monks who were traveling around to
the various centers for study could consider all under
heaven as their home and all within the four seas as their
house. At any time, in any place, they could lodge in Zen
cloisters or monasteries and stay there in retreat; all they
had to do was keep a single *hua-t'ou* in mind and concentrate on working at investigating it.

They would stay for a long time in a Zen hall, for a

year or six months, or for three or five years, or in extreme cases for ten years or twenty years, or even a whole lifetime, to investigate Zen thoroughly. Whether they had awakened or not, a *hua-t'ou* was always a *hua-t'ou*, and deliberate sitting to investigate Zen was always sitting to investigate Zen. The number of people like this were countless.

For this reason, after the full-scale development of Zen halls according to the monastic commune system, the real true life of wisdom of pristine Zen was gradually lost altogether. This was because the universal popularity of the fashion of investigating a *hua-t'ou* and staying permanently in a Zen hall caused the original Zen, that was based on transcendent wisdom and was the heart school of Buddhism, to change into a mode of Zen based on the meditation concentration of sitting Zen.

At this point, clinging fixedly to objects, they expanded the situational instructional method of the Sung dynasty Zen masters known as the three barriers, which thus became extremely popular. Thus evolved the tradition of calling "breaking through in investigation" the first barrier of understanding the mind, considering perception of essence to be the second barrier, and referring to the final realization of enlightenment as breaking through the final "impenetrable barrier."

In the early seventeenth century, at the beginning of the Ch'ing dynasty, the three barriers were given a special explanation in terms of the elemental analysis of the Only Consciousness school. According to this interpretation, breaking through the first barrier is the task of comprehending the ideational consciousness, breaking through the second barrier is the work of comprehending the seventh or mental consciousness, and breaking through the final "impenetrable barrier" is the task of comprehending the *alaya* or repository consciousness.

The reality behind all of this was that later students of Zen could not get completely free of the nest of meditational concentration states, and therefore they explained the states of meditation concentration in terms of a set of distinct realms of successive stages. Even if they merged with space, and all phenomena were within the mind, they were still revolving around within the field of mind, intellect, and consciousness, which means they had not gone beyond the mutually interdependent changes of body and mind.

I will refrain for the moment from giving a detailed analysis, for two reasons. One is that time does not permit it. The second is that not many have really and truly done work on the mind ground teaching of Zen and had experience in it.

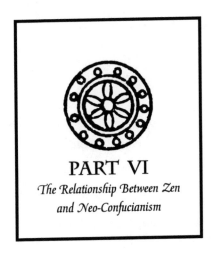

PART VI

*The Relationship Between Zen
and Neo-Confucianism*

CHAPTER 18

The Sources of Zen Buddhism's Influence on Neo-Confucianism

Generally speaking, whenever people talk about Zen, or study the source materials of the Zen school, they go to the records of sayings of the masters, or to books like the anthologies of recorded sayings such as the *Records of Transmission of the Lamp, Five Lamps Merged in the Source,* and *Records of Pointing at the Moon.* There they search out or admire the stories of the circumstances of the enlightenments of the masters, as well as the subtle impacts of the witticisms and pivotal sayings therein, and take these to be the workings of Zen, or the heart essence of the Zen school.

What they do not realize is that since Zen is called the heart of the mental source of Buddhism, it cannot be reasonable that no mention be made of all the practices of Buddhism, such as discipline, concentration, wisdom, and such refinements of action. Therefore, those who only recognized witticisms and arcane sayings as Zen entered into the decadence characteristic of the crazy Zen of Yuan, Ming, and later dynasties. In extreme cases this also caused the school of the Ming dynasty Confucian Wang Yang-ming to be accused of the same fault. At the same time, the decadence of the school of Wang Yang-ming in turn caused Zen to be repudiated on the same grounds.

In reality, if we would research the words and actions of those who attained enlightenment over the ages, all we have to do is to pay close attention to the biographical notes of the eminent monks and Zen worthies over the generations, as well as the book entitled *Zen Lessons*, which is devoted to notices from the records of the sayings and actions of Zen masters of the Sung dynasty. We can thereby understand how dignified and admirable was the example of the true Zen masters with regard to the practical cultivation of character and virtue. None of them engaged in pointless activities or uttered empty words, none of them talked only about witticisms and considered that to be Zen, and none of them considered only quiet sitting in silent awareness to be the ultimate teaching of Zen.

Furthermore, in this way it can also be understood how the Zen masters of the T'ang and Sung dynasties influenced the vital spirit of educational philosophy of the Chinese intelligentsia, how this influence played a role in the development of Chinese cultural thinking, and why it became a fundamental element in the formation of the Sung dynasty neo-Confucianism known as *Li Hsueh,* or the Study of Inner Design.

For the sake of convenience, I will bring up illustrations of Zen Buddhist thinking along with the theories of several great Confucians of the Northern Sung dynasty who founded the Inner Design movement of neo-Confucianism, and compare them so that everyone can know the sources of Zen Buddhism's influence on neo-Confucianism. But when I talk about influence and comparison, that does not mean exactly the same thing as making a copy or a reproduction: it is limited to the matter of influence and involves no intention of critically comparing them in terms of superiority and inferiority. On this point it must be made clear that I am adopting an attitude of cautious reserve.

In the historical records of the studies of the great neo-Confucians of the Sung dynasty, in every case it is noted that they "went in and out of Buddhism and Taoism" for several years. After this they seemed to wake up to their errors and considered entering Zen to be escapist, and considered entering Taoism to be fleeing society. So then they turned around and went into society, returning to Confucian thought, adopting the attitude that their responsibility was to cultivate themselves personally, order their families, govern their provinces, and pacify the whole land. But no matter how much they eventually rejected Buddhism and Taoism, in the course of their studies there were points at which they absorbed and amalgamated the two, which is an undeniable fact.

For example, take the theories of the neo-Confucian Chou Lien-hsi as expounded in his famous works *Comprehensive Writings* and *Explanation of the Diagram of the Great Ultimate*. If these works are read hastily, they seem to be entirely concerned with elucidating the appended traditions of the *I Ching* and the inner meanings of *The Doctrine of the Mean*. In reality, what Chou Lien-hsi does in these works is to amalgamate the doctrines and ideas of Buddhism and Taoism, particularly preferring the sort of primitive Taoism in which Confucianism and Taoism are not separated, and the philosophy of Lao-tzu.

Another example is the famous work of the great neo-Confucian Ch'eng Ming-tao (Ch'eng Hao), *On Stabilizing Nature*. It says, "What I call stabilization is stability in both action and stillness, without any sending forth or welcoming [an expression paraphrasing the Taoist classic Chuang-tzu], without any inside or outside. If you consider external things to be outside, and induce yourself to follow them, this is making your own nature out to have an inside and an outside. Furthermore, if you take your own nature to be following things externally, then when it is outside, what is inside? This is intending to cut off external seductions without realizing that one's nature has no inside or outside. Once you have set up inside and outside as two bases, then how can you suddenly talk about stabilization? . . . Now if one takes the mind that is averse to external things, and use it to seek illumination of some realm where there are no things, this is turning a mirror around and looking for a reflection on the back of it."

On the whole, sayings like this combine the inner meaning of Chuang-tzu's *Discourse on Equalizing Things* with the principles of the *Poem on the True Mind* by Seng Ts'an, the third patriarch of Zen. Here is his *Poem on the True Mind*:

> *The Ultimate Way is without difficulty,*
> *It's only averse to discrimination:*

Just do not hate or love,
And it will be thoroughly clear.
A hairsbreadth's miss
Is as the distance between sky and earth.
If you want to have it appear before you,
Don't keep conforming and opposing.
Opposition and conformity struggling
Become a sickness in the mind.
If you don't know the hidden truth
You work in vain at quieting thought.
It is round as space,
Without lack or excess.
It is indeed because of grasping and rejecting
That you are therefore not thus.
Do not pursue existing objects,
Do not dwell in forbearance of voidness:
In a uniformly equanimous heart
These quietly disappear of themselves.
Stop movement to return to stillness,
And stopping makes even more movement:
As long as you remain in dual extremes,
How can you know they're of one kind?
If you don't know they're of one kind,
You will lose efficacy in both realms.
Trying to get rid of existence is obscuring being;
Trying to follow emptiness is turning away from
    emptiness.
Much talk and much cogitation
Estranges you from it even more:
Stop talking and cogitating,
And you penetrate everywhere.
Return to the root and you get the essence;
Follow perceptions and you lose the source.

The instant you turn awareness around,
You transcend the emptiness before the eon.
Changes in the emptiness before us
All come from arbitrary views:
It is not necessary to seek reality,
All that is needed is ending the views.
Dualistic views do not abide;
Be careful not to pursue them.
As soon as there is affirmation and denial,
You lose your mind in confusion.
Two exist because of one;
Do not even keep the one.
When the one mind is unborn,
Myriad things have no fault.
No fault, no things;
Unborn, unminding.
When the subject disappears from objects,
Objects submerge along with the subject.
Objects are objects because of the subject,
The subject is the subject because of objects.
If you want to know them both,
They are basically one void.
One voidness the same in both
Equally contains myriad images.
If you do not see fine and coarse,
How could there be preference?
The Great Way is broad,
Without ease or difficulty.
Small views and foxy doubts
Slow you up the more you hurry.
If you cling to it, you lose measure
And will inevitably enter a false path.
Let it be as it naturally is;

Its body neither goes nor stays.
Let your nature merge with the Way,
And you will roam free of vexation.
Tying down thoughts goes against the real;
Oblivion is not good.
It is not good to belabor the spirit;
Why estrange the familiar?
If you want to gain the way of oneness,
Don't be averse to the six sense fields.
The six sense fields are not bad;
After all they're the same as true wakening.
The wise do not contrive;
Fools bind themselves.
Things are not different in themselves;
You arbitrarily get attached yourself.
If you take the mind to use the mind,
Is this not a big mistake?
When deluded, you create peace and chaos,
When enlightened, there is no good or bad.
All dualistic extremes
Come from subjective considerations.
Dreams, illusions, flowers in the air;
Why bother to grasp them?
Gain, loss, right, wrong;
Let them go all at once.
If the eyes do not sleep,
Dreams disappear of themselves.
If the mind does not differ,
All things are one suchness.
One suchness embodies the mystery,
Utterly still and unconditioned.
To see all things equally
Is to return again to the natural state.

Without any reason therefore,
You cannot judge or compare.
Stopping is movement without motion;
Movement is still without stopping:
Since both are not established,
How can one be such?
When you find out the ultimate consummation,
You do not keep rules and models.
When the mind in harmony is equanimous,
All doings come to rest.
When doubts are thoroughly cleared,
True belief is directly in tune.
Nothing at all stays;
There's nothing to fix in mind.
When open and clear, spontaneously aware,
You aren't wasting mental effort.
The realm that is not an object of thought
Cannot be assessed by conscious feelings.
The reality realm of true suchness
Has no other or self.
If you want to tune in right away,
Just speak of nonduality.
Nonduality is all the same;
There's nothing it doesn't contain.
The wise ones of the ten directions
All enter this source.
The source is neither expansive nor contracted;
One instant is ten thousand years.
There is nowhere that it is not;
The ten directions are right before the eyes.
The small is the same as the large;
You forget all about the bounds of objects.
The largest is the same as the small;

You do not see beyond it.
Being is none other than nonbeing,
Nonbeing is none other than being;
Anything that is not like this
Definitely should not be kept.
One is all,
All are one;
If you can just be like this,
What ruminations will not end?
The true mind is nondual,
Nonduality makes the mind true.
There's no more way to talk of it;
It is not past, or future, or present.

As for Ch'eng I's famous work *Four Guidelines*, apart from its treatment of the study of benevolence according to Confucius, its doctrines of inner and outer work seem very much like they are modeled on the didactic verses of Zen Master Chih-kung and others like him. The writings are too lengthy to quote here, so I would prefer to leave this to some time in the future when there is an opportunity to make a special study of this.

Coming to Chang Huang-ch'u (Chang Ts'ai), another early neo-Confucian, consider a famous saying of his such as, "Establish the mind for heaven and earth, establish direction for the people, continue discontinued studies for the sages of the past, open up great peace for ten thousand generations." Compare this with a saying of Hui-neng, the sixth patriarch of Zen, "Sentient beings are boundless; I vow to liberate them. Afflictions are endless; I vow to stop them. Ways into truth are infinite; I vow to study them. Buddhahood is supreme; I vow to fulfill it." From these two cases we can see they are on the same track, and it is only the wheels on their carts that are different. In addition to this, other famous writings of Chang Huang-ch'u can shed light on, and in turn be illumined by, the spirit and source message of the religious writings of Zen Master Ming-chiao Ch'i-sung. Consider, for instance, the following sayings of Master Ming-chiao.

First, "Nothing is more honorable than the Way, nothing is more beautiful than virtue. Where the virtue of the Way exists, even an ordinary man is not destitute; where the virtue of the Way does not exist, even if one rules the world one is not successful. Conscientious objectors of ancient times may have starved to death, but people today would all be glad to be compared to them. Tyrants of old may have been rulers of men, but people today would be angered if compared with them. Therefore students are concerned lest the virtue of the Way not fill them; they do not worry about not being in positions of power and authority."

Second, "The learning of sages and saints is certainly not fulfilled in one day. If the days are not enough, continue into the nights. Build it up over months and years, and it can be completed naturally. Therefore it is said, 'Study to accumulate it, question to understand it.' This means that without discerning questioning, study cannot lead to enlightenment. Wherever students go nowadays, there is rarely anyone who utters a single word to question others for discernment and understanding. I don't know how they will foster their spiritual state and achieve the benefit of daily renewal."

Third, "As the Grand Historian was reading Mencius, he unconsciously put the book down and sighed when he came to the place where King Hui of Liang asked Mencius, 'How will you profit my country?'

The historian said, 'Ah, profit is truly the beginning of disorder. That is why Confucius seldom spoke of profit, always shoring up the source.' The source is the beginning. Whether it is found among the upper classes or the lower classes, the degeneracy of lust for profit is basically the same. When those in public office profit unfairly, then the law is disordered. When those in the private sector profit by deception, then business is disordered. When business is disorderly, people are contentious and dissatisfied; when law is disorderly, the citizenry is resentful and disobedient. This is how people get to be so rebellious and belligerent that they don't care if they die. Is this not a demonstration of how 'Profit is truly the beginning of disorder'? The sages and saints were deeply cautious and aloof from profit, giving honor and precedence to humanity and justice. But in later times there were still those who deceived each other in hopes of profit; what limit is there to those who destroy morality and ruin education? How much the more serious is the problem when the path of adventurous profiteering is publicly espoused and pursued; under these conditions, how could we hope for the world's morals and customs to be upright, and not be thin and weak?"

Finally, Ming-chiao also said, "Of the evil that people do, there is that which has form and that which has no form. Formless evil injures people; evil with form kills people. The evil that harms people is relatively small; the evil that kills people is great. That is why 'there is poison in a party; there is spear and shield in talk and laughter; there are a tiger and a panther inside the chamber; there are savages in the next alley.' Unless you are yourself sagacious and nip these in the bud, guarding against them with standards of propriety, the harm they do will be considerable."

In the inner chapters of the famous work *Managing the World with Consummate Augustness,* Shao K'ang-chieh (Shao Yung), who is also considered one of the founders of neo-Confucianism, brings up a system of bases, assemblages, movements, and ages that he uses to figure out how to assess the past and know the future. This system has to do with the principles of assessing the changes of history and human affairs, as well as a way to represent the elements involved. This system, and the theories expounded in such works as his *Outer Chapters on Observing Things,* are in reality crystallizations of an amalgamation of the doctrines and ideas of Taoism and Buddhism, connecting them with the principles, images, and formulas of the *I Ching.* The three-dimensional cycle of bases, assemblages, movements, and ages repeats itself over and over again, turning into a focal point for examination of history and human affairs. This is none other than an application of the Buddhist principle of four eons of becoming, subsistence, decay, and emptiness to explain the logic of different stages in the worlds of humankind and other living beings. But Shao K'ang-chieh made Chinese history the central focus of his study and thus only calculated the process of small ages within a large age.

CHAPTER 19

*Neo-Confucianism and the Sayings
and Doings of the Zen Masters*

The previous quotations from Master Ming-chiao were concerned with the influence of Zen on the neo-Confucian thought of the Sung dynasty. Now I will select several examples of the sayings and doings of other Zen masters to bring to the attention of those who are researching Zen study and the neo-Confucian schools of the Sung and Ming dynasties. It is important not to take lip-service Zen or the subtle charm of Zen witticisms as the ultimate principle of Zen.

The Example of Master Yuan-t'ung Na

When Master Ta-chiao Lien first went to Mount Lu, Zen Master Yuan-t'ung Na, seeing him once, treated him as a person of great capacity for enlightenment. Someone asked

Yuan-t'ung how he recognized Ta-chiao. Yuan-t'ung replied, "This man is balanced and upright, not biased. Whether active or at rest, he is noble and dignified. Furthermore, in his study of the Way his actions are appropriate, and his words are simple yet logically complete. Whenever people have endowments like this, seldom do they fail to become vessels of enlightenment."

In 1134 the emperor of China sent a court messenger with a letter to Master Yuan-t'ung Na, summoning him to become abbot at the great monastery Hsiao-tzu. Yuan-t'ung claimed to be unwell and did not rise to the summons. Instead, he sent a message that Ta-chiao was worthy to respond to the imperial command.

Someone said to Yuan-t'ung, "The emperor shows reverence for the virtue of the Way, and his benevolence covers the land. Why do you insist on refusing?"

Yuan-t'ung said, "I am unworthy of monkhood, and my seeing and hearing are not clear. I am lucky to rest in the forest, eating vegetables and drinking water. There was that which even the Buddhas and patriarchs did not do, to say nothing of others. An ancient philosopher said, 'It is hard to live long with a great name; when will there ever be contentment?' Therefore the great poet Su Tung-p'o once said, 'If you know peace, then you thrive; if you know contentment, then you are rich.' "

Avoiding fame to perfect modesty and integrity, good in the beginning and good at the end; this was realized in Yuan-t'ung Na.

The Example of Old Man Shun

Ta-chiao said, "Old Man Shun was simple and straightforward by nature. He did not know about such things as weights and measures and the prices of goods. He had a daily routine that he never lessened or varied. Even things like lighting the lamps and sweeping the ground he did all by himself. He once said, 'An ancient has admonished us, "A day without work, a day without food." Who am I!' Even as he grew old, his will became increasingly firmer. Someone asked him why he did not employ a servant. Old Man Shun answered, 'In the cold and heat my rising and sitting is irregular, and I do not want to trouble anyone.' "

Old Man Shun said, "In transmitting and upholding this Way, what is important is true reality in everything. Distinguishing false from true, getting rid of deluded feelings, is reality in governing the mind. Knowing cause and effect, understanding fault and merit, is reality in practical behavior. Spreading the virtues of the Way, receiving those who come from all quarters, is reality in abbothood. Assessing talents and capabilities to nominate officials in charge of duties is reality in employing people. Examining words and deeds, determining whether or not they are appropriate, is reality in seeking the wise. If one does not maintain reality but only flaunts empty repute, there is no benefit for truth. Therefore in people's behavior it is only essential to be sincerely genuine; if you keep to this without changing, then even safety and danger can be as one."

The Example of Master Fu-shan Yuan

Master Fu-shan Yuan said, "The ancients associated with guides and selected companions, never letting themselves slack off at any time. They were never hesitant to work hard, immersing themselves in common labor, even doing chores like husking grain and preparing food. I experienced this fully in the course of my own apprenticeship. However, as soon as there is any consideration of whether you will get any profit or incur any loss, as soon as there is any comparison of gaining and losing, then there will be no end of wavering and compromise. And as long as you are personally not upright, how can you learn the Way?"

The Example of Master Wu-tsu Fa-Yen

Master Wu-tsu Fa-Yen observed, "In the monastic communities of present times, when students of the Way do not become known and are not trusted by people, it is usually because their conduct is not purely good and their efforts for people are not truly appropriate. They may suddenly grab for fame and profit, showing off their embellishments all over. So they are criticized by those in the know. This obscures the essential wonder of truth. Even if such people have buddhistic virtues, when heard or seen they will be doubted and mistrusted. If you have a roof over your head someday, you should remember this to make yourself work."

Wu-tsu Fa-yen continued, "When my teacher's teacher was first living at Yang-ch'i, the old building had broken beams and was barely enough to give shelter from the wind and rain. One winter night, snow and sleet covered the benches, so that there was no place to sit. The monks earnestly asked him to let it be repaired, but the old master put them off, saying, 'Buddha said, "In the time of the eon of decline, even the high cliffs and deep valleys are changing and inconstant. How can you have it all completely as you wish, seeking satisfaction for yourself?" You have all left home to study the Way, but your behavior is frivolous. You are already forty to fifty years old; how can you have leisure time to be concerned with a fine building?' And after all he did not consent."

Wu-tsu Fa-yen also said, "The ancients liked to hear about their own errors; they delighted in doing good; they were great in magnanimity, generous in concealing others' wrongs, humble in association with companions, diligent in helping and saving people. They did not let gain and loss divide their minds. Therefore their light was great, shining throughout all time."

The Example of Master Pai-Yun

Pai-yun said to Wu-tsu, "Many Zen followers with knowledge and ability see what has already happened but cannot see it before it happens. Cessation and contemplation, concentration and wisdom, guard beforehand. Doing, stopping, allowing, and extinction are noticed after they have already happened. Therefore it is easy to see what doing, stopping, allowing, and extinction use; while it is hard to know what cessation and contemplation and concentration and wisdom do. But the determination of the ancients was on the Way. They cut off thoughts before they sprouted. Even if there is cessation and contemplation, concentration and wisdom, doing, stopping, allowing, and extinction, all of it is a question of process. Therefore it has been said, 'If there is any talk about beginning and end, it is all self-deception.' This saying is that of an ancient master who saw all the way through and did not deceive himself."

The Example of Master Hui-t'ang

One day Hui-t'ang saw that Huang-lung appeared unhappy, so he asked him why. Huang-lung said, "I haven't found anyone yet who can be the accountant for the monastery."

Hui-t'ang then recommended the assistant superintendent Kan. Huang-lung shook his head, "Kan is still rough; I am afraid that petty people might intrigue against him."

Hui-t'ang suggested, "Attendant Hua is rather honest and prudent." Huang-lung considered, "Although Hua is honest and prudent, he is not as good as Hsiu, supervisor of the estate, who has capacity and faithfulness."

Ling-yuan once asked Hui-t'ang, "When Huang-lung needed an accountant, why did he give it so much thought?"

Hui-t'ang said, "Those with nations and those with families always have made this basic. Was it only Huang-lung who was like this? The ancient sages have also enjoined this."

Hui-t'ang explained to the imperial chamberlain Chu Shih-ying, "When I first entered the Way, I relied on myself very readily. Then after I saw my teacher Huang-lung, I retreated and considered my daily activities. I found that much in them was contradictory to the principle. So finally I worked on this for three years. Even in extreme cold and humid heat my will was unbending. Only after that did I finally manage to accord with the principle in all events. And now, every move I make is the living meaning of Zen."

Chu Shih-ying asked Hui-t'ang, "If a cultivated man

unfortunately makes a minor mistake, people who see or hear of it point it out unceasingly. Yet petty people do bad things all day long, but nobody considers it that way. What is the reason for that?"

Hui-t'ang replied, "The virtues of a cultivated man are comparable to a beautiful jade. If there is a flaw inside, it will inevitably show on the outside, so those who see it mention the anomaly, and cannot help pointing it out. As for petty people, everything they do in the daily activities is bad, so what is the need to speak of it?"

Another time he said, "The Way of sages is like sky and earth nurturing myriad beings, nothing left unprovided by the Way. The ways of ordinary people are like rivers, seas, mountains, streams, hills, valleys, plants, trees, and insects: each fulfills its own measure, and that is all. They do not know outside of that what is complete in everything. But could the Way be two? It is just that there turn out to be great and small because of depth and shallowness of realization."

Hui-t'ang also said, "What has been long neglected cannot be restored immediately. Ills that have been accumulating for a long time cannot be cleared away immediately. One cannot enjoy oneself forever. Human emotions cannot be just right. Calamity cannot be avoided by trying to run away from it. Anyone working as a teacher who has realized these five things can deal with the world without being troubled."

The Example of Master Huang-lung

Huang-lung said, "Essential to leadership is winning the community. Essential to winning the community is seeing into the hearts of the people. An ancient Buddha said,

'Human hearts are fields of blessings for the world, since this is where the path of reason comes from.' Therefore, the question of whether the time is obstructed or tranquil, whether something is deleterious or beneficial, always depends on human hearts. What is in people's hearts may be communicated or blocked; thence do obstruction and tranquility arise. Things are done with more or less care; thence do deleterious and beneficial conditions come about.

"Only sages can communicate with the hearts of all under heaven. Therefore in the hexagrams of the *I Ching*, when the sky trigram is below and the earth trigram is above, the resulting hexagram is called *tranquility*. When sky is above and earth is below, this hexagram is called *obstruction*. Symbolically, decreasing above and increasing below is called prosperity, while decreasing below and increasing above is called decline.

"Now if the sky is below and earth above, their positions are certainly contrary, yet it is called *tranquility*, because above and below are intermingling. If the host is above and the guest is positioned below, their meanings are certainly in accord, yet that is called *obstruction*, because above and below do not intermingle.

"So when heaven and earth do not intermingle, beings do not grow. If human hearts do not communicate, things are not harmonious. The meanings of decline and prosperity, decrease and increase, harm and benefit, also come from this. If people who are above others are able to control themselves and thereby be generous with those below, those below will gladly serve those above. Would this not be called beneficial? If those above slight those below and indulge themselves, those below will surely resent and oppose those above. Would this not be called deleterious?

"Thus when those above and those below intermingle, then there is tranquility; when they do not intermingle, then there is obstruction. Those who lessen themselves are a benefit to others; those who aggrandize themselves are harmful to others.

"How could the winning and losing of hearts be a simple matter? Ancient sages likened the human being to a boat, heart being the water: the water can carry the boat, and it can also overturn the boat. When the water goes with it, the boat floats, and when the water goes against it, the boat sinks.

"Therefore, when a leader wins people's hearts there is flourishing, and a leader that loses people's hearts is abandoned. Winning them completely means complete flourishing; losing them completely means complete rejection.

"So when both are good there are many blessings, and when both are bad the calamity is severe. Good and bad are of the same kind, just like pearls on a thread; flourishing and decline happen in this pattern, clear as the sun in the sky. This is a basic guide throughout the generations."

Huang-lung also once cautioned Wang An-shih, "Whatever you set your mind to do, you should always make the road before you wide open, so that all people may traverse it. This is the concern of a great man. If the way is so narrow as to be impassable, not only will that cause others to be unable to go on it, you yourself will have no place to set foot either."

He continued, "In what people say and leave unsaid, in what they do and leave undone, if they can say of themselves that they do not deceive heaven above, do not deceive other people outside, and do not deceive their own minds within, this can truly be called achievement. Still remaining careful about the hidden and the subtle when alone, if they find that there is ultimately no deception going on at all, then this can be called attainment."

Huang-lung told the recluse P'an Yen-chih, "The learning of sages and saints cannot be accomplished without care; it is essential to build it up cumulatively. Only by concentration and diligence, setting aside habitual desires, practicing it tirelessly, then extending and fulfilling it, is it possible to consummate that which is most sublime in the world."

P'an Yen-chih heard that Huang-lung's way of teaching was strict, so he asked him about the essentials. Huang-lung replied, "When the father is stern, the son is respectful; the guiding lessons of today are the models of the future. It is like leveling the ground, lowering where it is high and evening where it is concave. When they are going to climb up a mile-high mountain, I go along with them. When they get worn out and wind up in the abyss, I also accompany them. When their cleverness is used up and their illusions are ended, then they stop by themselves." He went on, "Cuddling and coddling are the means by which spring and summer give birth and nurture. Frosting and snowing are the means by which autumn and winter complete and mature. I want to say nothing, but how can I?"

The Example of Master Shui-an

Master Shui-an observed, "The *I Ching* says, 'An ideal person thinks of trouble and prevents it.' Therefore people of ancient times thought of the great trouble of birth and death and prevented it with the Way, until eventually the Way waxed great and was transmitted for a long time. People nowadays think that the vast distances of the search for the Way do not compare to the urgent immediacy of material interests. Because of this they view everything that passes in front of them through their habits of useless extravagance, calculating down to a hair tip, with opportunistic plans in their hearts. Therefore none can serve as guides for the whole year round, much less for considerations of life and death. This is why students are getting worse day by day, the communities are degenerating day by day, their unifying principles decline day by day, until they have reached a state of prostration and confusion from which they can hardly be saved. We must be aware."

PART VII
Zen and Chinese Literature

CHAPTER 20

Zen and the Evolution of the Realm of Ideas in Literature of the Sui and T'ang Dynasties and Thereafter

Chinese culture gradually deteriorated after the Wei and Chin dynasties, but it was at this time that Buddhist culture coming in from India and Central Asia suddenly provided Chinese thought with a transfusion of new blood. Out of this grew the dramatic rise of Buddhist studies from the time of the Northern and Southern dynasties through the Sui and T'ang dynasties. Thus the development of Chinese culture was formed on the basis of the three major traditions of Confucianism, Buddhism, and Taoism.

Zen, which rooted and flourished from the early T'ang dynasty onward, was like the vast flow of the water of the Yellow River, a powerful torrent that entered deeply everywhere into each and every part of Chinese culture. Whether formally or formlessly, directly or in a roundabout way, its enriching influence has been received in all times and all places. It certainly has had the effect of "carrying along the oars of the travelers in the rivers, watering the fields of the people as it comes out of the mountain crags." I will cite some simple abbreviated examples of the most obvious cases, adding explanations to provide material for research into the relationship between Zen and the development of Chinese culture.

If we speak of Chinese culture from the point of view of literature, we might grasp the essentials simply and categorize them summarily by using the era as a background and the particularly well-developed genre to represent it. Then we find a process of development from Han dynasty prose to T'ang dynasty poetry, to Sung dynasty lyrics, to Yuan dynasty drama, to Ming dynasty novels, to Ch'ing dynasty linked rhymes and plays.

From the late Han through the T'ang dynasty, in essays, elegies, poetry, and song, the traditional contents and realms of ideas in Chinese literature generally have their roots in the five classics, go in and out of the principles of Confucius and Mencius, and swim in the beauties of the various philosophers to form a central realm of ideas in literary expression. Occasionally, works are outstanding, for example the serene realms of thought in the literary output of Lao-tzu, Chuang-tzu, and the Taoist spiritual immortals.

The one special feature of Chinese literature between the times of the Northern and Southern dynasties and the Sui and T'ang dynasties that has always been overlooked by scholars of Chinese literary history is the importation of Buddhist thought, which instigated massive translation projects to render its scriptures and classics into Chinese. Through the initial efforts of such distinguished monks as Hui-yuan, Tao-an, Kumarajiva, and Seng-chao, a special class of Chinese Buddhist literature developed whose subsequent influence remained unchanged over more than a thousand years.

This is a truly rare phenomenon, something that has hardly any parallel. But because the ordinary literati of later times were not really familiar with the principles and classic sources of Buddhism, they insisted on their ignorance as knowledge, and considered whatever they did not know to be unworthy of consideration; thus they excluded Buddhist works from their study. This great flower of Chinese literature was thus buried in oblivion. As the Zen masters have said, "Our eyes are originally clear, but are blinded by teachers." This is most regrettable.

Poetry

I will just refer to the representative works of the T'ang dynasty to discuss the stylistic evolution of T'ang poetry. First came the so-called Ching-lung period literature of the early T'ang dynasty, from Shang-kuan T'i to the four great poets Wang Po, Yang Ch'iung, Lu Chao-lin, and Luo Pin-wang, on through Chen Ch'uan-ch'i, Tu Shen-yen, and Sung Chih-wen, the outstanding poets of the time of Empress Wu (684–705). This poetry still had some of the remaining influence of the Sui dynasty, as well as the new simplicity of style of the early T'ang dynasty.

Later there was a change in the literature characteristic of the K'ai-yuan and T'ien-pao eras (713–755). Exemplary poets of that time were Li Po, Tu Fu, Wang

Wei, Meng Hao-jan, Kao Shih, Ts'en Ts'an, Wei Ying-wu, and Liu Ch'ang-ch'ing. Then there were the so-called ten geniuses of the Ta-li period (766–775). These poets very clearly and obviously added elements of Buddhism and Zen to their works.

Another change transpired with the poetic forms of the Yuan-ho and Ch'ang-ch'ing eras (806–823). As examples of writers who were representative of the standards of the age and leaders of fashion, we might mention the accessible Po Chu-i and the stylish and charming Yuan Chen, as well as Meng Hsiao, Ku T'ao, Chang Chi, and Yao Ho.

Finally, in late T'ang dynasty literature there were poets such as Tu Mu, Wen Ting-ch'un, Li Shang-yin, and others like them, all of whom were involved in Buddhism and Taoism to some extent. The flavor of Zen permeated all of them and this is what enabled them to produce the special breath of fragrance and enduring lyricism characteristic of T'ang poetry. As to the nonsecular works of eminent monks, they may be considered exceptions in the literary tradition of T'ang dynasty poetry and are generally not recognized by orthodox poets. Nevertheless they have their own independent value.

A few poems are particularly inclined toward the temperament of Zen and are excellent examples of T'ang dynasty literature and the influence of Zen philosophy.

In the works of the poet Wang Wei, for instance, there are long verses of Zen sayings:

Verses on the Pure Body

Once you arouse the slightest material thought,
There lies the body like morning dew.

When you look at the clusters and elements thus,
Where can you place self and person?
Confronting being, one's surely the host;
Heading for emptiness, why abandon the guest?
Purifying the mind, why interpret intellectually?
Enlightenment is the ford of delusion.
Illness arises as a result of attachment;
Through craving, one starts to feel poor.
Form and sound are not others' delusions;
Ephemeral mirages are my reality.
Reaching in all directions, what is missed?
How can myriad differences defile?
The barbarian just sleeps on a high pillow;
In the stillness and silence, what neighbors are there?
The war won, he doesn't scheme for food;
Order established, he gladly carries kindling.
If you are never different,
Who talks of far or near?
The ephemeral void goes uselessly on and on,
Floating existence reaches steadily into the distance.
There is no vehicle and no rider;
As it is said, wisdom's humanity's boat.
How can we abandon the realm of poverty and illness
And not be wearied on the current of life and death?
No problem if you are like a horse;
Let me be an ox.
Planting blessings, I give thanks to Kasyapa;
Seeking humanity, I laugh at Confucius.
On what harbor are oars not plied?
On what road are carts not pushed?
I reflect on the learned and thoughtful;
Why are so many so far away?

Flowers gathering and dispersing in empty space,
The trees of afflictions are now sparse, now thick.
Annihilate thought, and you become indifferent;
Sit on purpose and you are being ambitious.
Conquering Wu, go back to Shu;
Don't criticize if you haven't arrived.

And here are several examples from Po Chu-i:

Self-Understanding

They say a certain poet was a Zen student in a
*   former lifetime,*
And another says he must have been an artist in a
*   past existence.*
I too gaze upon my past lives when I am in a trance:
My debt of many lives has been song and poetry;
If it were not so, why would I sing and recite madly
Even more after getting sick than before getting sick?

Reading a Zen Scripture

We must know that all appearances are not what
*   they appear to be;*
And if we dwell in remainderless nirvana, then
*   there still is a remainder.*
Forget words at the words, and you
*   comprehend all at once;*
Talk of dreams in a dream is double layers of vacuity.
Can you seek fruit along with flowers in the sky?
How do you look for fish in a mirage?
If controlling movement is meditation,
*   meditation moves;*
Not meditating, not moving, this is suchness as is.

Two Verses on Feeling Uplifted

*Luck and misfortune, calamity and blessing, have
    their sources;
It is only necessary to know them deeply, not to
    worry about them.
I have only seen fiery light burning splendid houses,
I have never heard of wind and waves
    overturning an empty boat.
Honor is a public instrument, of which not much
    is to be taken;
Profit is a personal disaster, which should be little
    sought.
While different from a gourd, it is hard not to eat;
On the whole, it's best to stop as soon as you've
    eaten enough.
If fish can enter the depths, why worry about hooks?
If birds can fly high, they won't hit the nets.
If you scramble to warm your hands first where
    it's hot,
You're helpless no matter what you do, when you
    have regrets.
Having summoned a bowl of orangutan blood
    into the honored presence,
You try to grab a moment's ease nesting on a tent.
I have one saying that you should remember:
There are many people in the world who bring
    bitterness on themselves.*

As for the poetry of an unconventional eminent monk such as the Cold Mountain Man, the loftiness of its realm of ideas enters into the Zen realm of the inconceivable, but its accessibility is superior to that of the layman Po Chu-i for it completely embodies the popular sensibility.

Since the poetry of the Cold Mountain Man (the famous monk Han-Shan) is generally familiar to everyone, I will quote only one of his poems below. The rest are typical of poet monk poems of the T'ang dynasty, among which there are certainly a number of very good works. For example, here are some verses of the poet monk Ling-i:

Looking for Mount T'ien-mu After a Rain, Asking About the Valley Road

Last night clouds rose east of the ceiling of heaven;
In the spring mountains it rained and the wind blew.
The forest flowers fell, to flow down with the
*   valley stream;*
I want to go up to Dragon Lake, but I don't
*   know if I can get through.*

On a Monk's Cloister

The moon leads me through the valley of tigers;
The snowy pine branches are draped with ivy.
In the endless green mountains, my journey's almost
*   done;*
Where the white clouds are deep, old monks are many.

Stopping by to See an Adept on the Way Back to Mount Ts'en

A Zen traveler mindlessly remembering the artemisia,
The path he travels naturally turns often toward
*   the mountains.*
I know you want to ask about the affairs of the
*   human world,*

That is why I have passed this way along with the
floating clouds.

Then there are examples from the poet monk Ling-ch'e:

In a Monastery, Replying to a Government Official

Having grown old, my heart is uncluttered, free
from external concerns;
My hempen robe and straw sandals too are just
enough to suit me.
Whenever we meet you always say it would be
better to give up office;
But when have I ever seen anyone in the forest?

On Hearing of the Death of an Independent Scholar

From time to time I hear of the death of old friends;
Every day I lament this aging body of mine.
For white hairs not to grow must be impossible.
To whom does the eternal presence of the green
mountains belong?

In addition to these, although I will refrain from quoting them for lack of space, many of the works of poet monks like Kuan-hsiu and Hsiao-jan of the T'ang dynasty have earned undying fame.

Poetic literature influenced by the Zen state of mind became even more distinguished in the Sung dynasty. In the early Sung, nine famous poet monks inspired poets fascinated by Zen study to develop the famous Hsi-k'un style. Famous literati such as Su Tung-p'o and Wang An-shih were also influenced by Zen thought, with the result that they composed works of purity and beauty beyond the ordinary.

After the capital of Sung dynasty China was moved to the south, four more great authors had inextricable ties to Buddhist and Zen thought: Lu Fang-weng, Fan Ch'eng-ta, Yang Wan-li, and Kou Hsieh. But they were all more inclined to the literary aspect of writing, so I will not go too far off the subject to discuss them in particular. Therefore, I will just pick out some of the more accessible poems of distinguished Zen monks of the Sung through Ming dynasties to serve as a brief introduction. For example, here are some poems by Tao-chi, a popular figure of the Sung dynasty:

> *How many times have I boarded a boat alone on*
>   *West Lake?*
> *The boatman, knowing me, does not talk about the fare.*
> *The cry of a calling bird breaks the recondite silence;*
> *Here the line of mountains goes down into the glow.*
> *The spring light on the lake has broken its reticence;*
> *The willows on the lakeshore brush the carved*
>   *balustrades.*
> *I calculate there's no need for a single penny to buy it;*
> *It's given over to this mountain monk strolling*
>   *back and forth.*
>
> *The red brocade of the shoreline peach blossoms*
>   *stands out,*
> *The green threads of the willows on the bank are light;*
> *In the distance I see white herons looking for the fish,*
> *Plunging through the point of blue of the placid lake.*
>
> *In the fifth month the West Lake is cool as autumn;*
> *New lotuses spew blossoms, floating fragrant in*
>   *the dark.*
> *Next year, when the flowers fall, where will the*

people be?
Wine jug in hand, I ask the flowers, and the flowers nod.

There are also other unique works by this author, such as the following poem:

Sixty years of slovenly misbehavior;
The east wall knocks down the west wall.
Gathering it all back in now,
As before the water is blue to the horizon.

If we talk about the quality of poetry in terms of poetic realms, Tao-chi's work is in no way inferior to that of Fang Ch'eng-ta or Lu Fang-weng, who were among the four great poets of the Sung dynasty. If we talk about poetry in terms of Zen states, there is virtually not a single line in Tao-chi's work, not a single word, that does not express a state of Zen. If one does not have decades of deep experience in Zen insight and work, it is really not easy to discern the point.

Here are also some examples of Zen-influenced poetry by Wang An-shih:

Immovability

Immovable action is goodness in action,
The flow of ignorance has a current.
Every sort is born, abides, and passes away;
With every thought I learn, think, and practice.
Ultimately not bound up in principles,
Neither do I don the garb of a monk.

Dreams

If you know the world is like a dream, you seek
nothing;

When you seek nothing, your mind is everywhere
    empty and calm.
Then it is like pursuing dreaming states in a dream,
Fulfilling countless dream virtues.

The Mouth of the Chiang-ning Valley

The moon descends into the floating clouds, the
    water recedes into space;
On the banks of the clear water, the night
    greets the fifth watch wind.
How can the grasses and trees on the northern
    mountains be seen?
Dreams ended, I toss and turn under the dim lamp light.

Striking sail at the river mouth, the moon in the
    yellow dusk;
The little shop, without a lamp, is about to close
    its doors.
Half sticking out on the shoreline sands, the maple's
    about to die;
Of the moored boats there still remain the marks
    of the year gone by.

To the Dharma Master Tao-kuang of the Azure Cliff

All things remote, at ease, the mind knows itself;
Being brazen in the world increases one's slipups.
Moving my bed I turn alone to the autumn wind;
Lying there I watch the spiders weaving their webs.

Spring snow in Ta-liang fills the city with mud;
One horse is always gazing at the return of the
    setting sun.

> *Knowing myself and the world, I laugh to myself*
>   *after all;*
> *Long, long have been these thirty-nine years of*
>   *mistakes.*

There are also some relevant examples from the poetry of Fan Ch'eng-ta:

> *Unpredictable changes take place in a trice;*
> *How pitiful the multitude of the superficial and shallow!*
> *Heaven has no cold or heat, nor has it any seasons;*
> *Humanity is not hot or cool, not having worldly*
>   *feelings.*
> *All flitting about turns out to be but so many butterfly*
>   *dreams;*
> *Off in the distance, how many roosters can there be*
>   *crowing?*
> *Red dust billows by the side of the ice mountain;*
> *Unobstructed by extravagant buildings, the moon*
>   *and frost are clear.*

> *I know for sure all things are fundamentally empty,*
> *Yet I still serve worldly influences with my mind.*
> *When adverse or pleasing situations appear, joy and*
>   *anxiety change;*
> *Tsk, tsk! Who is the real master in charge?*

> *Myriad cedars stand in a row, with banners of blue-green*
>   *clouds;*
> *Softly, gently wafts the scent borne by the evening*
>   *breeze.*
> *Dust hits the face of the travelers below the mountain;*
> *Who would know there is clarity and cool in the*
>   *world?*

A few outstanding poems by Zen masters of the T'ang and Sung dynasties will reveal the key to the evolution of the style of T'ang and Sung poetic literature. For instance, here is the awaited example by the Cold Mountain Man, the Great Master Han-shan:

> *My mind is like the autumn moon,*
> *Clear, bright, and pure in the azure pond.*
> *There is nothing that can compare to it;*
> *How would you have me explain?*

By Zen Master Hui-wen, we have the following example:

> *A dreamlike illusory body of fifty-five years:*
> *East, west, south, north—which is closest?*
> *The white clouds completely dispersed beyond*
>   *the thousand mountains.*
> *In the endless autumn sky, the crescent moon is new.*

By Zen Master Hui-chung:

> *Many years in the dust and dirt, I am spontaneously*
>   *buoyant;*
> *Though I wear a monastic robe, I am not yet a monk.*
> *Today I have returned to fulfill my original aspiration;*
> *Yet I still keep my hair, waiting for the Burning*
>   *Lamp Buddha.*

Several examples by Zen Master Hsueh-tou Ch'ung-hsien:

On Not Conforming to the Times

> *The laymen of noble families, I do not wish to visit;*
> *For now I find it best to nestle in the crags.*
> *The great lake is thirty-six thousand acres broad;*

*The moon is in the heart of the waves, but who is
there to tell?*

The Lion of Wu-lao Peak

*Crouching on the ground, dancing in the air, its power
unending,
Why should its claws and fangs compete in the trends of
the time?
Heaven had it born above a thousand peaks;
It rears its head even though it does not get lifted up by
the clouds.*

An Expression of Passing Through the Absolute

*When a single leaf drifts in the air, right then you see
it's autumn;
The absolute must be passed through, to the noisy chatter:
Next year again there will be new regulations,
Disturbing the spring breeze, ultimately never ending.*

Great Success Is Not Domineering

*The peak of Ox Head Mountain is locked in multilayered
clouds;
The master sits alone in silence, lodging this body.
The hundred birds do not come, and spring passes again;
Who knows who will go to the hermitage?*

Enjoying Myself in Concealment

*I've made a picture of the beloved lake and garden of
yesteryear,
The seventy-two peaks reflected green in the heart of the
waves.
Now I lie in seclusion, thinking of things of the past;
I've added a figure of myself leaning on a stone wall.*

Sending Off a Zennist Going to T'ien-t'ai

*The spring wind blows away the sea and mountain
    clouds;*
*All night there is utter stillness and quiet, no neighbors
    around at all.*
*The moon is at the stone bridge, there is no other
    moon;*
*Who knows who the man at the edge of the moon could
    be?*

Sent to a Scholar

Finding fire in water—how deep is that doctrine?
A fistful of straw, after all, is not actually gold.
Do not say that Chuang-tzu knew how to equalize things;
How many people have ultimately arrived at unminding?

A Fisherman

*Springtime sunlight moving along, the mist on the
    banks is light;*
*The surface of the water windless, a fishing boat goes
    across.*
The reel of a thousand feet of line lies in the heart;
Who knows where the giant fish can be caught?

Apart from these examples, among the works of Ming
dynasty Zen poet monks, for metrical precision and refinement of both Zen and poetic expression, none compare
with those of Zen Master Yu-t'ang on living in the mountains. Here are five examples of his work:

In front of a thousand-fathom cliff, I lean on my staff;
Effort should ultimately arrive at effortlessness.
Words if uttered unreasonably pollute the clear sky;

Action improperly cultivated is a flaw in a pure jewel.
How can one metaphor comprehend all things?
When the sheep is lost, it's useless to weep at the
crossroads alone;
The Wayfarer Hsia-hsi has eyebrows white as snow;
Knocking at his door under the moon, I present some
purple mushrooms.

Where the irregular current ends, I stake out a
hidden abode;
A single tree forms a bridge across the little valley stream.
As the peaches bloom in the spring rain, I remember
ancient Taoists;
As the wild peas grow in the evening mountains, I
dream of purists of old.
On the way looking for a monk, I come to the north of
the stone bridge;
Awaiting the moon, I suddenly think of the west of the
pillar of heaven.
Let me ask about what it is the wise men of old achieved;
For ten years I've galloped on horseback to hear the
rooster crow at dawn.

The red sun of the human world readily sets in the West;
Don't be proud of myriad skills and undertakings at all.
If it has no flaws when split from the matrix, only then
is it a gem;
If a drawing turns out to have legs, then it is not a snake.
With the night rain in the green forest, the ferns uncurl
their fronds;
With the spring breeze in the emerald trees, the flowers
open their hearts.
If every trace of worldly thought is not completely melted,
The shortcut to honor and fame is in the haze and mist.

Desolate, deserted is the Way; to whom shall I speak
of it?
Alone, I close my cottage door, day turns to evening
again.
Before the six senses are divided, who is agitated and
disturbed?
As soon as one element stirs, there is naturally
confusion.
In the empty forest the rain stops, a crow calls its mate;
In the shadowy valley the wind is cold, a tiger roars at
the herds.
Censuring tyrants, praising sages, feelings are not yet
ended;
Having a body, I have managed to get to lie in the
deep clouds.

Stop right now if you are going to stop;
For what do you seek fame after death?
When the world is chaotic, the martialists' strategies
are unfolded;
When talents are lofty, the judgments of critical writers
arise.
Cutting wood in a backwater is a perennial regret;
Sailing off on the ocean in a raft is a universal sentiment.
Who knows deathlike Zen, the chilly nighttime moon;
The stone couch at the root of the pine is level and
even.

Later we come to a Ming dynasty poet monk like Ts'ang-hsueh who was not only a leader in both religious and secular literary worlds of his time, but was also a folk poet, and could even be called a mendicant patriot poet. He was one of the last of the old survivors of the end of the Ming dynasty who fled into Zen to escape society.

However, he was secretly active as a defender of the nation, working for the restoration of Chinese autonomy. He wrote many famous poems, too numerous to mention. A few of the most poetically and spiritually elevated of his compositions are representative:

> *No one under the pines, one game is left;*
> *Pinecones fall onto the chessboard.*
> *Spiritual immortals even have spiritual immortal moves;*
> *Forever and ever winning and losing are never completely*
>   *finished.*

> *How many times have I stood in the snow, enveloped*
>   *in clouds?*
> *Having used up all diligent effort, I will learn from*
>   *the lazy;*
> *Even if dragged by a rope through the nose, I still*
>   *will not rise,*
> *A free individual in the depths of the river mists.*

> *Raising my head beyond the skies,*
> *I see there are no clouds;*
> *Who is like us in the human world?*
> *Through thorny thickets,*
> *I walk with free strides;*
> *Under a moonlit curtain,*
> *I hide my body in the dark.*

Ts'ang-hsueh also wrote a poem to the famous poet Ch'ien Yu-shan (Chien-yi) when the latter took to concentrating solely on Buddhist literature after his library burned down, and this is worthwhile to cite:

A fondness for dealing with worldly matters is like a
  gambling game;
Sleeping soundly in the forest is left up to an old man.
The will of heaven has not allowed you to finish little
  writings;
When the river is clear, after all you want to see the
  unrecovered pearl.
If you do not face north, how can you know Han?
Looking to the eastern mountains, there is only Yu.
Before finishing with the famous novels, you delve
  into the Buddhist canon;
All the writings of the human world might as well
  be burnt to naught.

If we have some training in history and read this poem, we can understand how Ch'ien Chien-yi could serve two courts, the Ming and the Ch'ing. We can also understand how he researched materials relating to the secret activities of the surviving elders of the late Ming to write a Ming history that would attract the loyalties of the surviving descendants of the dynasty. We can also understand the circumstances of the burning of his library and the process through which he came to concentrate on Buddhist studies. Then we can sense the great mastery of Ts'ang-hsueh in this poem using Zen language, with every line and every word containing hidden potential.

In the foregoing examples, having spoken of how the poetry of the T'ang dynasty evolved under the influence of Zen, I hastily mentioned the Sung and Ming dynasties, but I have only introduced a few of the essentials. This was to explain how Chinese literature from the Sui and T'ang dynasties onward absorbed the meditative vistas of Zen, which made the accomplishments of the

T'ang and Sung poets possible. The purpose of this is to draw the attention of those who are studying the relationship between Zen and Chinese literature.

As to the relationship between Buddhist literature from the T'ang and Sung dynasties onward and Chinese prose and rhetoric, it is even greater, but there is no need to talk much about it. The important point is that well-known works such as those of the famous literatus Su Tung-p'o have an extremely intimate and obvious connection with Zen and Taoist thought, and that is precisely how there came to be such an incomparable literary realm of ideas.

Lyrics and Songs

The characteristic fashion of poetry that developed in the T'ang dynasty changed with the birth of lyrical literature during the late T'ang and the Five dynasties. Following this trend, beginning in the late T'ang dynasty through the Five dynasties, the Zen masters of the subsequent Sung, Yuan, Ming, and Ch'ing dynasties used lyrics to expound Zen; and both their lyrics and their Zen were very good. Unfortunately, they have simply been neglected. For reference I will cite some of the works of lyricists who have always been highly respected and publicly recognized.

For example, there are the lyrical works by Hsin Chia-hsuan, such as the following.

On the Road to Stone Gate

The waterfall up in the mountains spews tons of pearls;
Over a thousand-fathom precipice, the flying squirrels
  descend.

*Though I've taken a woodcutters' path, I find the way is
    blocked;*
*It seems there are people's voices, but when I listen
    there are none.*
Away from the log bridges, far from the Buddhist monks,
*There's a reed hut in the tall bamboo south of the valley
    stream;*
*Don't be averse to the wanderer who keeps coming and
    going;*
This place is most suitable to house an elderly man.

Things at Hand on Arising from Sleep

The water plants bob unevenly on the azure ripples;
Snakelike shadows in the pond reflect a group of frogs.
*Due to the wind the wild cranes still dance although
    they're hungry;*
*With too much rain, the mountain mulberries are sick
    and do not flower.*
Where there is name and profit, there are many wars;
*With petty disputes at the door, there is fighting every
    day.*
They do not know there also is a dreamland paradise;
I wake from my dream to find the sun has not yet set.

Feelings

Origins have naturally never been equal;
It is only the last car that brings the venerable one back.
Who knows that in the silent empty mountains
*There are high-minded people writing poems on picking
    out flowers?*
*The yellow chrysanthemums are young, the evening
    scents disperse;*
Everywhere alike it is the time for picking out blossoms.

The bees work a lot harder than bureaucrats do;
The butterflies fly freely amongst the flowers.

On Obeying a Directive to Retire
and Accept a Sinecure Serving in an Imperial Chapel

The elderly retire; who ever talked of clinging to office?
Today I have been pardoned; the kindness of the
    emperor is magnanimous.
So I light incense sticks, a real chaplain;
I also string together writings, an old palace guard.
Bracing my aching legs, I wash my sagging face;
How quickly I've gone from being an old invalid
Into the guise of officialdom;
It is easy for me personally to forget all about the world,
But after all it is still hard to get the world to forget
    about me.

A Casual Composition on Climbing Hill and Vale

Don't linger on the autumn scenery, roaming under the
    flowers,
Or else you must be prepared for the sadness of fallen
    blossoms.
For a hundred years the rain beats down, the wind
    blows away;
Of ten thousand affairs, scant three are normal, two
    are fully all right.
Taking unease and handing it over to worry,
This life in the world itself has no anxiety.
New sadnesses thrown away one after another,
I want to accompany the spring back to the end of the
    sky.

Partridges of Good Omen: A Casual Composition on Rising from Convalescence in the Capital to Climb Up to a Taoist Cloister

In the days I was young I feared people would know
  my name and reputation;
Now that I have grown old, I find my way of life
  differs from what I had wished.

The wild grasses of yore once called me on a remote
  aspiration;
Old acquaintances now have lodgings to which to return.
Who can find out the way to pacify the mind?
A traveler comes to the cloister, shutting down the
  working of his power;
What a laugh, he makes you unable to find out what
  he is like.
Over the vast expanse of the clear river, white gulls are
  flying.

When will confusion and agitation ever cease?
Ever since I came out of the mountains I have not
  been free.
On an autumn moon night in a cloister overlooking
  autumn waters,
Chrysanthemums blossom in autumn around the
  hall of hovering clouds.
The principle of going along with conditions should
  be understood;
Too much recognition is not to be forcibly sought.
First is one's own individual being, with sadness unended;
Then there is adding sadness to sadness.

As for Ming dynasty songs, here are some examples by Liu Ping-chung:

Dry Lotus Leaves

Dry lotus leaves, their color green,
Their old stems wave in the wind.
The clear fragrance lessening,
Yellow is added,
All because of last night's single frost;
Deep silence lies on the autumn river.

Also,

Dry lotus leaves, their color not much,
Cannot help breaking in the wind and frost.
They cling to the autumn waves,
Their stems sticking up in the air.
Palace beauties sing in chorus
Lotus-picking songs;
The luxuriant flowers pass in a dream.

Then there are the songs of Ho Hsi-ts'un, such as the following:

The name and profit of the cities and courts is hardly
  relevant;
Experiences of success and failure are not that familiar.
Don't say no one knows the true from the counterfeit.
Here is where it is happening;
As the hurried flow surges ahead, who can control it?
A pair of swift eyes, a fine fellow,
Doesn't see Rich Springtime Mountain.

When you turn your head around, you find
The glory and disgrace of past and present are vain;
All of it is a roust.

I say an empty reputation isn't fit for use;
I urge the heroic to minimize the troubles before them.
The palaces of Ch'in, the tombs of Han:
Cloudlike dreams on the Raven River
Arouse the autumn wind as of old.

Ever since the apricots bloomed
The weather hasn't been clear,
Spoiling the sightseers' fun.
Scarlet snowflakes come flying,
Filling the fragrant pathways.
What about the springtime orioles?
When the orioles aren't chattering,
The wind settles down.
The wine jug has feelings;
The night is cool, the people quiet,
Singing stops at Drunken Elders' Inn.

There are also the songs of Hsien-yu Chu-chin, such as:

Tzu-ling of the Han dynasty, Yuan-ming of the Ch'in
    dynasty;
Both men perfume the literary world even up to now.
Who mentions an old man fishing,
Who names an old man farming?
Their activities are equally light.
At the Manor of Five Willows,
The moon is bright, the wind is clear;
On the Seven Mile shoreline, the waves are calm, the
    lake is placid.
Bending at the waist, the heart is already embarrassed;
Stretching out the legs, dreams are early awakened.
Listen to the judgments of the sages and saints
Over myriad ages.

In the beginning of the Ch'ing dynasty there was a famous young lyricist named Na-lan Hsing-te, who was a talented scion of the Manchu nobility then ruling China. Here are three examples of his lyrics:

Huan-shao Valley

Fallen leaves fill the valley, the water is already freezing,
But the evening sun still shines on the inn.
The abandoned temple along the way has lost its
    nameplate;
Stopping their horses, travelers gaze at the writing
    on the tablet.
Hearing the cock crow, people put out the lamps
    in front of the Buddha;
Toiling and laboring, the world of dust; when will
    they ever wake up?

Swallows nest in the empty rafters, the painted walls
    are cold;
The flower rain of the heavens is scattered in the dark
    passes;
The curling incense smoke and the sound of scripture
    reciting
Hover between being and nonbeing.
Butterflies passing through the shadows of the screens,
The cherries and plums are half-eaten by the birds;
At this moment, faced with this, I am at a loss for words.

If there is no way to toss it off, bitterness grows more
    and more.
Clouds of mercy bow to life restoring incense;
Try to figure out the talk of the sublime lotus blossoms.
Just let the wishes of all sentient beings be fulfilled;

Where else would you apply thought?
The curling smoke and the flickering lamp both rend
  the heart.

Novels

In Chinese literature, novels are inseparable from T'ang dynasty plays and lyrical songs, and their contents are similar to those of Chinese drama. For nearly one or two thousand years they have always been intimately connected with the philosophies and sentiments of Taoism and Buddhism. For this reason a popular saying developed about the composition of drama in later ages, "If there is not enough drama, the Immortals and Buddhas will perform."

To place this topic in a fitting format, for the moment I will divide the evolution of the writing of Chinese novels into two major stages. The first stage starts with the tales of gods and spirits in the legends of high antiquity and continues through the allegories and symbol stories in the writings of the philosophers of the Chou and Ch'in dynasties. It culminates in works such as the traditional records of spiritual immortals transmitted by the Taoists from the Han and Chin dynasties, writings such as *The Tradition of the Harmonious Son of Heaven*, *The Unofficial Record of the Martial Emperor of Han*, *The Legend of the Queen Mother of the West*, and so on. Most of these have traditional cultural ideas mixed with elements of Taoist sentiments and fantasies of spiritual immortals.

The second stage begins with the anecdotal novels of the T'ang dynasty and morality tales from Buddhist scriptures, goes on through the drama of the Sung and Yuan

dynasties, and finally comes to the essays and belles let-
tres of the Ming and Ch'ing dynasties. Most of these
works contain the sensibilities of Buddhist and Taoist
thought, and in the background there is often more in the
way of Buddhist thought and feeling than of Taoist.

It is worth taking special notice of the fact that
no matter whether it be a novel or a play, and whether
it be a happy story, a sad story, or a light comedy, or even
an erotic work, the final conclusion of the piece inevitably plays itself out and winds up according to an
author's own moral rules. Those rules were a combination of Buddhist and Taoist ideas, defining patterns of
cause and effect relationships in human life and things
of the world. If we were to describe old-fashioned novels
and plays in satirical terms, we might say they generally
conclude with, "The maid is presented with gold in the
late-blooming garden; the nobleman in difficulties passes
the government exam." They expound the evident and
ineluctable principle of cause and effect in an individual
human life. Because of the philosophical milieu of their
time, the short stories of T'ang dynasty writers bore the
influence of Zen and Buddhism, so they of course had
already started this trend. It was not until the Yuan and
Ming dynasties, however, that it really became a fixed
standard embedded in the contents of every story, and
evolved into a stilted model for fiction writing.

Between the Yuan and Ming dynasties, writers of
historical novels such as Luo Kuan-chung, who wrote the
pioneering *Tales of the Three Kingdoms*, would start out
with a verse to open up the source and clarify the meaning, expressing the idea of the cycle of cause and effect in
history, and making a general comment on the philosophy
of history. For example:

> *Roiling, roiling, the water of the Long River as it*
>   *runs to the east;*
> *The flowers on the waves have washed away all the*
>   *heroes:*
> *Right and wrong, success and defeat;*
> *When you turn your head around, you find they are*
>   *empty.*
> *The green mountains are still there as of yore;*
> *How many times has the evening sun grown scarlet?*
> *The white-haired fisherfolk and woodcutters on the*
>   *river banks*
> *Are used to watching the autumn moon and spring breeze.*
> *With a jug of unfiltered wine, a joyful get-together;*
> *How many affairs of past and present*
> *Are given over to a laughing conversation!*

From the standpoint of philosophy, this poem by Luo Kuan-chung bespeaks the teaching of the Buddhist *Diamond Cutter Scripture*, in which it says, "All compounded things are like dreams, illusions, bubbles, reflections; they are like dew, like lightning—you should observe them in this way." This is the best explanatory note to the literary realm expressed by the author. It is also just like a poem by Zen Master Kao Pu-k'un on what transcends the absolute:

> *Last night the rain drenching the inn*
> *Knocked down the grape arbor:*
> *The superintendent called out the workers*
> *To try to brace it up:*
> *They tried to hold it up till dawn,*
> *But it's as pitiful as before.*

Is this not a work that breathes through the same nostril?

This inspired someone later to compose a novel based upon this kind of thought. It is *Tales of the Three Kingdoms*, which expounds on events that resulted from the rule of consequences in the cycle of causes and effects of political division and strife.

Another famous work is by Shih Nai-an, entitled *Legend of the Water's Edge*. If you just read this novel superficially for its surface content, it seems to be no more than a description of social unrest from the Sung to Ming dynasties, with officials fooling their superiors and keeping those below them in ignorance, cheating and oppressing the farmers, and arousing a sympathetic reaction in response to injustice and unrest. If you read more deeply, however, you will find that it has not departed from the central philosophy of the causes and effects of good and evil, or the idea, implicit or explicit, that the strong and powerful are not allowed to die well. Later, one author feared that people would misunderstand, so a book appeared called *Record of Wiping Out Brigands*. Although this book was written with good intentions, one cannot help but feel that it was unnecessary, like drawing legs on a picture of a snake.

Other books such as *Journey to the West* and *Neutralizing the Spirits* consist entirely of Buddhist and Taoist thought, so I will not talk about them here. In addition, historical novels such as *Records of the States of Eastern Chou* and *Tales of the Sui and T'ang Dynasties* contain the idea of not being blind to cause and effect, which is central to Buddhism and Zen. This is just like the following poem of Zen Master T'ien-mu Li on the saying of the *Surangama sutra,* "If that which is not attributed to you is not you, who is it?"

If it is not attributable to you, then who is it?
The lingering scarlet leaves falling fill the fishing beach:
As the sun sets, the wind stirs, nobody sweeps them;
The sparrows, taking them in their beaks, fly over the
edge of the water.

The development of fiction continued along these lines through the Ch'ing dynasty with the work of the famous essayist Pu Sung-ling, *Liang-chai Record of Oddities.* This consists almost entirely of stories about vixens, ghosts, and spiritual entities that throw the causal relationships of good and evil into relief. This type of theme is even more pronounced in *Awakening the World about Marital Relations,* an outstanding work illustrating the Buddhist idea of cause and effect over the passage of generations. This book explains the troubles and afflictions of relationships between men and women, between husbands and wives, in the course of human life.

Such thinking had already become pervasive throughout popular society. That is why the following verse was hung at the gate of the imperial shrine in Hangchow around the time of the end of the Ch'ing dynasty and the beginning of the Republican era, drawing out this concept:

Husbands and wives have been connected in the past;
Whether their connections were good or bad,
Those connections never fail to meet.
Sons and daughters are basically past debts:
Whether seeking repayment or making repayment,
They only come on account of debt.

Coming to the world of the famous, among the vernacular novels written in reaction to the old cultural style, the book *Dream of the Red Chamber* depicts the lifestyle of the great families of noble clans. This book has been interpreted arbitrarily and subjectively by many people in modern times who have become fascinated with it and treated it as an individual field of study in itself.

The Dream of the Red Chamber starts with a Buddhist monk and a Taoist priest, each of whom sings some words of warning for the materialistic world. It goes on to talk about all sorts of entangling feelings and emotions, and how they are all recorded in the ledger of the realm of illusion of cosmic space, which seems to be real but is like a mirage, set on the other shore of a vast ocean of misery, throwing into sharp relief the Zen state in which the goal of salvation is not far from the empty flowers of dreamlike illusions.

In the author's apologia at the beginning of the book he says, "Pages full of wild words, a handful of bitter tears: all will say the author is mad; who understands the savor therein?" He also says by way of admonition, "When the artificial is real, the real is also artificial; where nothing is something, something is then nothing." Is this not a good explanation of the sayings in the *Surangama sutra*, "With pure thought you fly; with pure emotion you fall," and "Birth exists based on consciousness; extinction is removed through form"?

That is why some people read *The Dream of the Red Chamber* as a good book to help them attain enlightenment, yet others mistakenly enter into the novel's bedazzling sensuality. The question of gain and loss and right and wrong is all in the thought of the individual concerned.

CHAPTER 21

The Importance of the Relationship of Zen and Literature

Among the examples I have introduced from T'ang dynasty poetry, Sung dynasty lyrics, and Yuan dynasty drama, some are not completely mixed with Buddhist and Zen expressions, but evolved and developed out of Zen mental states; if we just look at them from the surface, it might not be easy to perceive the intimate connection between Zen Buddhism and the evolution of Chinese literature.

Actually, I have just picked out a few works of clear beauty and austere elegance related to Zen mental states to make a cooling, thirst-quenching concoction for the agitated and disturbed human life in the toilsome realm of dust of this time in this world. Zen originally does not set up writings and does not have to make pompous use of literature to show how lofty it is; yet Zen and the Zen masters from the T'ang and Sung dynasties onward all formed a tight relationship with literature, becoming as it were virtually inseparable. Two additional explanations will help you understand the importance of the relationship between Zen and literature.

The Significance of Poetry

When Confucius in his later years edited the classics of poetry and documents, determined rites and music, and thus formulated the intellectual system of traditional Chinese culture, why did he use poems to make his point, discussing them again and again, quoting them from time to time? And why did the Confucians from the Ch'in and Han dynasties onward change things around to make the *Book of Odes* first among the five classics, before the *Book of Documents, I Ching, Book of Rites,* and *Spring and Autumn Annals?*

It is because the spirit of the traditional culture of the Chinese people has always been completely centered on human culture. Although it also has elements of religious thought, it is not like the pristine culture of the West, which derives completely from theological religious thought; the foundation of human culture naturally is not apart from human thought and emotion, the inner and outer functions of the body and mind.

Religion can be used to arrange people's thoughts and emotions, taking them on an eternal road into the distance and to an inconceivable realm so that they may attain the effect of individual peace of mind. But if you approach the faith of religious thought purely from the standpoint of human culture, sometimes it may function only emotionally.

Therefore, when you want to adjust human emotions, it is necessary to have a kind of literary art that can transcend the mental realm between apparent reality and the emotions. Only then is it possible for emotion and thought to sublimate themselves to a state of mind similar to a religious state, whereby it is possible to transcend the environment of apparent reality. Feelings and thoughts are set elsewhere, developed to become independent and autonomous, so that it is possible to arrange your own heaven and earth.

In the popular culture of China, strong emphasis has always been placed on the value of poetry, a literary genre that has been a shining light throughout history. The ancients who lauded the role of poetry in maintaining the fiber of society only knew that it was so without knowing why it was so; they had not deeply studied the value and subtle function of the states engendered by poetic lyrics.

Among the Chinese intelligentsia of the past, poetry, history, philosophy, music, and the arts were all inseparable parts of a total curriculum. That is why most literati fifty or sixty years ago naturally knew how to compose poetry and lyrics, the only differences between their works and those of antiquity being their quality and depth. These writers were so versatile that it is hard to make strict distinctions among poets, scholars, philosophers, politicians, and military scientists in old China. They were individuals who could easily master other fields of learning, and whose lives were not restricted to poetry.

Zen not only does not set up written words; it also has formlessness as its gateless gate of entry. To put it another way, the state of Zen is a stateless state, shedding formal doctrines of religion, and emphasizing the true spirit of practice and realization of Buddhism, sublimating the mental experience of human life and entering into a realm of pure clarity, the open consciousness that has no form yet is all forms.

For the purposes of expediency in expression and explanation, I have no choice but to use a method of making something out of nothing, bringing up examples of scholarship in order to compare them with the realm of Zen. Thus there are the subtle mental realms of poetry and lyrics, of the most developed of the fine arts, and of the highest martial arts; these subtle mental realms can be compared with Zen to some degree.

That is why even the extemporaneous verses, lyrics, and writings of the Zen masters of the T'ang and Sung dynasties were all literary works of the finest caliber and profoundest depth. Thus the spreading of this fashion gradually formed the intellectual realm of T'ang, Sung, Yuan, Ming, and Ch'ing dynasty literature, and the unique style of Chinese literature of the past.

The Significance of Religion

Religion and literature are originally an inseparable continuity. Whatever the religion, it can spread throughout society and form an enduring character of its own, influencing each era and each class of society through the course of history, because it depends entirely on the highest value of its doctrine formulated into literature. Only when religion rises from the level of popular folklore to be refined and sublimated into the highest realm of literature can its life and history continue on forever.

Aside from the fact that the doctrines of Buddhism themselves contain religious, philosophical, scientific, artistic, and academic thought, with abundant material of great value on all of these facets of knowledge, the main reason why its doctrines and the life of wisdom of Zen were able to strike roots, sprout, flower, and flourish in the milieu of Chinese culture was because after Buddhism was imported into China, it developed a special independent literature that went on to influence the nerve centers of all of Chinese culture. Take, for example, the New and Old Testaments of the Bible. Among the peoples of the Western countries of each and every different language into which it has been translated, the Bible has had exceedingly great authoritative literary value. Therefore, speaking in terms of its worth as literature, without making an issue of its doctrinal contents, it can also be said of the Bible that its "literary expression and realm of ideas are sufficient for a thousand years."

I always say to friends of different religious faiths that if they want to think of a thousand years, they must pay careful attention to their doctrines and their literature. This is because of my observation that even though religious faiths are not the same, and the question remains about the depth and truth of each religious doctrine, nevertheless the basic element that qualifies anything to be called religion is that it encourages people to be good and do good, and aims to save the world and the human mind from perennial troubles.

These are good things that several great religions share in common. We do not have to quarrel over differences regarding what might be the ultimate and highest philosophy of religion, clinging possessively to our own views until we reach the point where the power of religion dies out. That is a mistake made by human cultures and civilizations in the past; it is also a weak point in the psychology and mentation of the human race, and a shameful disgrace as well.

Summing up, as far as the relationship between Zen and Chinese literature is concerned, in reality the connection is much too deep and intimate to tell the whole story. In a brief space I have cited examples of a few T'ang dynasty poems, Sung dynasty lyrics, Yuan dynasty dramas, and Ming dynasty novels to show the Zen influence. I did not go deeply enough into them, but just brought up some of those that happened to occur to me from memory. I urge everyone to think their implications through, so that they may arrive at the states indicated therein.

So, in general, the influence of Zen on Chinese literature has been substantial, and through this literary influence Zen has also acted to shape the nation. Throughout the ages the great Zen masters have tried to help humanity by directly pointing to the root essence of matter and mind via a "transmission outside of scripture." Although their pointing was in a most direct fashion, the side effects of this directness have been various cultural waves penetrating every segment of Chinese society and culture. One need not say there was Zen "in all times and all places" to maintain that it has had a profound influence on the nation; one need only trace through some of the indications given to understand the story of Chinese Zen and its influence on China.

1312